# The Wisdom of the Hindus

*The Wisdom of the Vedic Hymns, the Brahmanas, the Upanishads, the Maha Bharata and Ramayana, the Bhagavad Gita, the Vedanta and Yoga Philosophies. Wisdom from the Ancient and Modern Literature of India*

Edited, and with an Introduction

By

**Brian Brown**

*Editor of "The Wisdom of the Chinese"*

Foreword by

**Jagadish Chandra Chatterji**

B.A. (Cantab), Vidya-Varidhi. Head of the Department of Sanscrit Research in the Government of His Highness the Maharaja Gaekwar of Baroda, India. Author of "Hindu Ideals," etc.

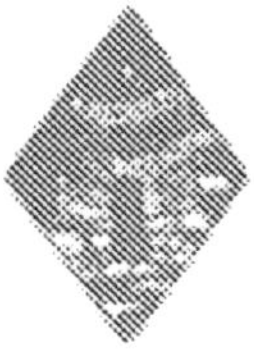

NEVER the Spirit was born;
The Spirit shall cease to be never;
Never was time it was not;
End and beginning are dreams!

BIRTHLESS, and deathless, and changeless,
Remaineth the Spirit for ever;
Death hath not touched it at all,
Dead though the house of it seems!
*From "The Song Celestial" (Bhagavad Gita)*

# INTRODUCTION

MAX MULLER in his "India, What Can It Teach Us" says:

"If I were to look over the whole world to find out the country most richly endowed with all the wealth, power and beauty that nature can bestow — in some facts a very paradise on earth — I should point to India. If I were asked under what sky the human mind has most fully developed some of its choicest gifts, has most deeply pondered on the greatest problems of life, and has found solutions of some of them which well deserve the attention even of those who have studied Plato and Kant — I should point to India.

"And if I were to ask myself from what literature we, here in Europe, we who have been nurtured almost exclusively on the thoughts of the Greeks and Romans, and of one Semitic race, the Jewish, may draw that corrective which is most wanted in order to make our inner life more perfect, more comprehensive, more universal, in fact more truly human, a life not for this life only, but a transfigured and eternal life — again I should point to India."

Who are the people of India, and where did they come from? In ancient times, about 325 B.C., when the Greeks under Alexander the Great invaded what is now called India, they found in the northwestern part a river, which the natives called Sindhu. The Greeks in their language transformed the name to Hindus and Indus.

Then, as time went on, the word, which was originally Sindhus, — and which, according to some authorities, means divider, but according to late research is said to mean a flow or flood, — underwent a gradual change, until it finally became India and the people Indians.

Historians tell us that these people are a branch of the great Aryan family consisting of seven races: Hindus, Persians, Greeks, Romans, Celts, Teutons, and Slavs. All emigrated from their ancestral home in Asia. The Celts, Teutons, and Slavs are supposed to have entered Europe on the northern side of the Caucasus and Caspian Sea. We find this reference in the Code of Manu, who might be called the Moses of the Indo-Aryans, for the "Book of Manu" is their great moral code.

The land that lies between the two mountains is named Aryávarta, or land of the Aryans. The word Aryan means superior or best, and Varta means land. So it seems the rightful name of India would be Aryavarta. The original home of these Aryans is thought to be in central Asia, and when the family separated the Indo-Aryans came southward from the headwaters of the river Oxus and entered what is now called India, sometime about 2500 B.C. India is the central one of the three great peninsulas of southern Asia. On the north is the mountain region of the Himalayas, below which are the vast and fertile river plains, watered by the Indus, the Ganges, and

INTRODUCTION xi

other streams. On the south, separated from the Ganges by the Vindya range, is the hilly mountain tract called the Deccan, or South.

The history of India opens with the struggle between the Aryan invaders and the original inhabitants. Who the native inhabitants were is not quite clear since they left but few monuments, which throw little if any light on their origin as a race. Professor V. A. Smith, in his "History of India" says:

"Some day, perhaps, the history of Dravidian civilization may be written by a competent scholar, skilled in all the lore and language required for the study of the subject. Early Indian history, as a whole, cannot be viewed in true perspective until the non-Aryan institutions of the South receive adequate treatment."

The Aryan invaders, who were no doubt tall and fair, entered through western India and later on gradually spread to other parts, separating themselves sharply from the non-Aryan, dark-skinned, early inhabitants of India. While living in the valley of the Indus they composed the hymns of the "Rig-Veda," their most ancient literature, which embodied their racial myths, the story of their wanderings, and their spiritual aspirations. Like the Greeks, another branch of the Aryan family, they offered these hymns to their gods. No other people ever produced a body of religious poetry of such striking originality and beauty, at such an early stage of their history. Without books, without preachers, without pulpits, they reflected upon the natural phenomena, and sang with divine inspiration to the great spirit.

Indeed, the entire race consciousness of the Hindu is concerned with spiritual knowledge of how all things in the universe came into existence and for what purpose. Thus the term Rig-Veda literally means spiritual cosmology in verse, the word Rig meaning verse — Veda knowledge — and the two in conjunction symbolizing spiritual knowledge in verse.

At this period the institution of the family was the foundation of their society and the father was the spiritual director of the household. He offered up all prayers and directed all the spiritual exercises. From this phase of social and religious organization, a part of the ancient Vedic religion, with numerous gods, the Hindus gradually came under the control of a body of priests, called the Brahmans. The Brahmans succeeded in placing Vedic interpretation upon a philosophic basis, which involved the worship of the triad, Brahma, the Creator, Vishnu, the Preserver, and Siva, the Destroyer.

The Brahmans absolutely dominated the life in India. Nothing could be done without their sanction; they were omnipotent. They in turn made anthologies from the "Rig-Veda," which were called the "Yajurs," — "Black and White," — and were used in some of th ˙ ˙ces; in fact, the "Black and White Yaju           nanus for the Brahmanic priests, containing the same precepts, but differing in their arrangement.

Later a collection made from the same source was called the "Sama Veda," that is, "Veda with Melodies," for these hymns were arranged for chanting at the offerings to the God Indra.

A fourth collection called the "Atharva-Veda," was made much later than the others and is more popular, for it contains common practices, superstitions, and folklore. The subsequent Vedas, according to scholars, may be distinguished by additions to the source material of the original Rig-Veda. For example, the Brahmans later on produced a literature of their own, which was really an attempt to interpret the Vedas to their fullest extent. This literature was called the "Brahmanas," or "Sayings of the Brahmans," and was the beginning of the works called "Aranyakas" or "Forest Books" and the early "Upanishads." The "Brahmanas" might be described as the "Hindu Talmud," for they interpreted for the people the early writings of the Hindus, as the Talmud explained the early writings of the Jews.

The "Aryanakas," meaning belonging to the forest, were written by holy men, who removed themselves from the world of practicality to the spiritual thought world for concentration upon life's problems. These truths, the fruit of meditation in the forests of India, were the source of the "Upanishads," next to the "Rig-Veda" the most important literary production of Vedic India.

The "Upanishads," or Esoteric Doctrine, literally, a sitting down to meditate and think out, represent a final understanding of the mystic sense of the Vedas. It answers questions on the origin of the universe, the nature of God, the nature of the Soul and the connection between mind and matter. The "Upanishads" are really the foundation of the "Vedanta" (meaning end of the Vedas) philosophy, in fact, they are the beginning of the metaphysical inquiry, which ended in the full development of Hindu philosophy.

We have seen that the creed, or philosophy, which these forest philosophers thought out, contained the essence of a new religion, that led away from the old Vedic gods. In the "Upanishads" there is only one real existence in the universe, the Supreme Brahman, Atman or Self, and all creatures are the manifestation of this Self. The doctrine taught, is: that no material thing may be loved for itself, but for the soul that is manifest in it; from that manifestation of Self or Soul can be obtained a knowledge of God and a release from the cycle of births and deaths. This is based upon the Law of Karma, or cause and effect. Your cause was bad! Your effect will be bad! Therefore, you must be reincarnated until your activity is on the spiritual plane. Then your actions or work will be all in the spiritual thought-world and rebirth is not necessary, for you are absorbed into the all-divine essence.

## INTRODUCTION

The great phrases used, are: "Thou art that," — "I am Brahman," — and "I am He," — phrases which probably mean: "You are a part of the great spirit and I am a part of the great spirit; we are all of the Divine." This is the earliest form of Vedanta philosophy. The influence of deeds on rebirth led these people to the abolition of desire, since desire led to selfishness, which in turn caused rebirth and recurring suffering and kept the wheel of pain turning forever. In fact, all the six systems of Indian Philosophy are based upon the eradication of evil passions that the soul may be freed from rebirth.

A careful study of these six systems of Indian Philosophy shows that they contain the highest truths known to the ancient Greeks. Pythagoras, Thales, and Parmenides were indebted to the early Hindu Sages. Modern philosophy likewise has drawn inspiration from the same spring. Sir Monier Williams, in his "Brahmanism and Hinduism," says: "Indeed, if I may be allowed the anachronism, the Hindus were Spinozites more than two thousand years before Spinoza, Darwinians many centuries before Darwin, and evolutionists many centuries before any word like evolution existed in any language in the world."

The Samkhya system, the oldest of the six philosophies of India, was founded by a sage named Kapila. I have pointed out that the ancient Vedic religion passed into monism and then into the worship of a triad, Brahma, Vishnu, and Siva.

xvi INTRODUCTION

Kapila disagreed with all this on a basis of rationalism, for he saw only the diversity and not the unity of the universe. In his hypothesis he denies existence of a creator and ruler of the universe and he considers the world developed from matter, according to certain laws. He believed that a subtle substance was later imparted to it, out of which the internal organs of all creatures were formed; all psychic sensations, thinking, feeling; in fact, all sense perception, according to the Samkhya doctrine, are purely mechanical processes of these internal organs. This would appear as if Kapila thought that the soul, or this subtle substance, is the consciousness, though not a morally responsible substance. The object of the Samkhya philosophy was to teach people the distinction between the soul and matter, and when they knew that, the necessity for being reincarnated passed away. In this way the Samkhya philosophy supplied the foundation upon which most of the ancient philosophies are built and which gave rise to the idea of evolution later used by various schools of Platonists. Professor E. W. Hopkins says: "Plato is full of Samkhya thought, worked out by him, but taken from Pythagoras."

The Yoga system, founded by Patanjali, is the Samkhya metaphysics combined with bodily and mental exercises, and the conception of the personal God. Patanjali held that mysterious powers can be acquired by asceticism and turning away from the world by concentration upon the inner Self, through which the highest spiritual development can be reached. He taught, moreover, that psychic breathing helps to attain this ideal.

The Vedanta system is divided into two schools. The earlier was organized by Jaimini and the later by Badarayan. The object of both is to teach the art of reasoning for the express purpose of interpreting the Vedas. The earlier school is sometimes called the Purva-Mimansa, or First Investigation, and describes what works of devotion and sacrifices merit the reward of heaven. The second school or Uttara Mimansa is called the Later Investigation and is today the most popular philosophy in India. Apropos of this point Swami Abhedananda in his book "India and Her People" says: "Since the decline of Buddhism in India the Vedanta has become most prominent and most powerful, having a large following among all classes of people, from the Priest down to the Pariah."

The chief teacher of Vedanta philosophy was Sankara, who tells us that this doctrine proceeds from an eternal Being, and eternal Principle, Brahma, there is only one being in the universe, God or Brahma, and all else is Maya, or illusion. The wise man transmutes all things of sense into spiritual things and contemplates that One Spirit, who resembles pure Space.

The Vaisishika system was founded by a sage named Kanada, a contemporary of Buddha's about 500 B.C. His philosophy is called the Atomic System, for it traces the origin of the universe to a combination of atoms and molecules. It is very remarkable to find that Kanada spoke of molecular motion, expansion and contraction, and the like, centuries before the Greeks.

The Nyaya system, formulated by Buddha, is sometimes called a system of logic, but it combines logic with philosophy, since it is based upon the atomic theory of Kanada. Buddhism is no longer alive in India, the land of its birth, but thrives in many other countries, including China, Japan, Ceylon, and Siam. There are two schools of Buddhism, Mahayana, or Great Path, which worships Buddha as God, and Hinayana, or Humble Path, which considers Buddha a superior man. On account of the vastness of Buddha literature I have not included any selections in this anthology. Brief excerpts would not do Buddhism justice. It merits treatment separately.

In Indian literature, the "Maha-Bharata" and the "Ramayana," the two great epics, are comparable with the "Iliad" and "Odyssey" of the Greeks. The "Maha-Bharata," or the great war of the Bharatas, is supposed to have been fought in the thirteenth or fourteenth century before Christ. The leading subject of the poem is the war between the Kauravas and the Pandavas who descended, through the Bharatas, from the Puru, the great ancestor of one branch of the lesser race.

The object of the struggle was to get possession of the capital city, Hastinapur. There are many memorable episodes and passages in the "Maha-Bharata," including the wonderful philosophical poem, the "Bhagavad-Gita" or "Lord's Song." This poem is the noblest and purest expression of Hinduism in existence. The unknown author shows himself to be a great spiritual poet and philosopher, with a universal outlook. In the "Maha-Bharata" we find also the story of Krishna, the Hindu Christ, here described as the reincarnation of Vishnu by a miraculous birth. He performs miracles and is regarded as the Redeemer of the world. The selections from the "Bhagavad-Gita" in this anthology are taken from Sir Edwin Arnold's beautiful translation, the "Song Celestial."

The "Ramayana," or the "Wanderings of Rama," was written by the sage, Valmiki. The "Ramayana" celebrates the life and exploits of Rama — the love of Rama and his wife Sita, the abduction of Sita by Ravana, the demon king of Ceylon, and the war carried on by Rama for her rescue. The introduction to the "Ramayana" says: "He who reads and repeats this holy lifegiving 'Ramayana' is liberated from all his sins and exalted with all his posterity to the highest heaven."

Like all the other great poems, born of race imagination and experience, the Indian epics have a value beyond their historical or allegoric significance. They give us an insight into the manners and customs of their age, beautified by the imagination of the people. I have used the admirable translation of Romesh Dutt, which, for keeping the continuity of the story and for beauty of expression cannot be equalled. I have condensed as much as possible, giving thereby the outline of the story with all its symbolism of thought and poetry.

The "Hitopadesa," or "Good Advice," is a collection of ethical tales and fables, all pointing a moral, and compiled from a larger and older work, called "Pancha-tantra." The verses herein used are translated by Sir Edwin Arnold and the aphorisms by the Abbé Dubois.

In this introduction, we have discussed the six systems of Indian Philosophy. All philosophical systems, however, are wrought on three main sources. The body or sense perception gives rise to materialistic philosophies, the head or mind to rationalistic philosophies, and the heart or soul to idealistic philosophies. The Hindus have united these three conceptions in the aspiration of the human soul to realize its immortal birth. To the Hindu spirit is the reality, and living for spirit is the only life. For that reason material things do not interest him; the writing of history in so far as it involves the recording of mere events is not a national characteristic; time and things of the earth are of small account.

## INTRODUCTION

These great spiritual forces produced among the Hindus many great thinkers and moral leaders. Centuries before Plato wrote, or Pericles ruled, they had a practical system of government, while in the sphere of philosophy they rose to a height of speculation attained by few of the later Europeans. They were, for example, among the first of the races to proclaim the brotherhood of man.

Nanak, the founder of the Sikh religion, said, "God will not ask man of what race he is. He will ask him, What have you done?" Herein we may see the genesis of the present tendency presented by this Indian seer. Indeed, the psychic factor dominated their civilization when the other races were still groping about for a spirit to quicken their imagination and direct their steps.

All of the spiritual sages mentioned in this anthology are among the foremost men the Indian nation has produced. Like Swami Vivekananda, from whose "Inspired Talks" and "Raja Yoga" I have quoted, they marked eras in their respective religions although one and all taught the "Fatherhood of God and the Brotherhood of Man." One of these objects realized would of course bring about a natural fulfillment of the other. If, moreover, the psychic factor ever grows strong enough in our civilization to place our efforts on a spiritual basis, both will be realized. Chaunder Sen prophesies that this sought-for spirituality will develop in Western civilization, and will unite us in bonds of sympathy and comprehension with the great religious heritage of the East:

"The future religion of the world will be the common religion of all nations, but in each nation it will have an indigenous growth and assume a distinctive and peculiar character. No country will borrow or mechanically imitate the religion of another country; but from the depths of the life of each nation its future church will grow up. In common with all other nations and communities, we shall embrace the theistic worship, creed, and gospel of the future church. But we shall do this on a strictly national and Indian style. One religion shall be acknowledged by all men; one God shall be worshipped throughout the length and breadth of the world; the same spirit of faith and love shall pervade all hearts; all nations shall dwell together in the Father's house; yet each shall have its own peculiar and free mode of action. There shall, in short, be unity of spirit, but diversity of forms; one body, but different limbs; one vast community with members laboring in different ways, and according to their respective resources and peculiar tastes, to advance their common cause, 'The Fatherhood of God and the Brotherhood of Man.'"

BRIAN BROWN.

## FOREWORD

TO THE Western World India has always been a land of mystery; a land full of unintelligible systems of beliefs and puzzling philosophies, when, as a matter of fact, the principal ideal back of all Indian thought can be reduced to a very simple explanation. The Material body is the great enemy of the Soul's Salvation and the Senses are the misdirecting sign-posts that cause us to build our plans for life upon the material plane. So every system of Indian philosophy points beyond the Material, and endeavors to transcend it, to find pure spirit and reality. This does not mean that the world does not exist as an object, but that, as far as its being ultimate reality is concerned, it could not be — for only the Spirit essence back of it is, in the finality, definable as reality.

Through the ages the things that have actuated Man the most have been, and still are, in their very nature, deep mysteries. Man has, more or less vaguely, felt the power of these mysteries but they have ever eluded complete comprehension by him in his limited capacity as an individual.

These mysteries reside in Man's innermost self as the most supremely impelling forces. It was this truth, expressed by our ancient seers and sages in the Veda and Upanishads, that led the Indian mind to the belief that the Spiritual is the all — in the first, in the now, and in the last. It was thus that the Hindu mind was able to surrender the object world of matter. In the construction of the spiritual principle every phase of finite experiences was denied, as being non-reality, and called "Illusion." When the ultimate consideration of matter is reached, and that can only be accomplished by transcending this illusion of Matter, then the Soul can be released from the compelling contact with the unreal and be absorbed into the spiritual essence, which is pure truth and ultimate reality.

The Western mind, unfortunately, does not quite understand what the Indian philosophy means in its definition of reality, and is inclined to think that it teaches that there is no external universe at all. Such is not the case. What the Indian philosophy teaches is, that as for the universe being absolute reality, that is an illusion, for the finite mind cannot conceive absolute reality.

We are, all of us, the accumulated experiences of the races down the ages, to which is added our spiritual light — the Soul — that all-powerful substance, which in the finite gives prophetic vision to comprehend the infinite through spiritual emotion and to place upon its altars the ideals to that end. The ideals of India, as expressed in the ancient literature, have been handed down as a heritage. Western scholars have explored and translated much and the result of their noble work is to be had — though not easily available to the average man, for the volumes are in most cases expensive, very often technical and difficult. This objection Mr. Brown has planned to overcome by selecting some of the finest sections of the Indian literature and giving them the proper arrangement in order that the person without any knowledge of the subject may easily become familiar with the literature of ancient and modern India. It is high time that every endeavor was made to make known to the Western World the wisdom of India, for if we read the writings and historical accounts left by Pliny, Strabo, Herodotus, Porphyry and many other ancient writers of different countries, we shall see how highly the civilization of India was regarded by them. In fact, between the years 1500 and 500 B.C., the people of India were so far advanced in religion, metaphysics, philosophy, science, art, music, and medicine, that no other nation could stand as their rival, or compete with them in any of these branches of knowledge. My earnest prayer, therefore, is that this book of gleanings from what has been realized by the Hindus as truth in their lives may prove to be of real help to all who may have the good fortune to read it. It is a garland of Eastern thought-flowers.

May it be a real blessing to all by whom it may be worn, and may it bring peace and happiness to all who may inhale its fragrance. I can find no better closing than to quote what Tennyson said:

> "Let the East and the West without a breath
> Mix their dim lights like life and death
> To broaden into boundless day."

Shubham astu
Sarva-Jagatām
JAGADISH CHRANDRA CHATTERJI

LONDON, ENGLAND
August 15, 1921

# The Wisdom of the Hindus

## RIG-VEDA

### Creation

THEN there was no entity nor non-entity; no world, no sky, nor aught above it; nothing anywhere, involving or involved; nor water deep and dangerous. Death was not, and therefore no immortality, nor distinction of day or night.

BUT THAT ONE breathed calmly alone with Nature, her who is sustained within him. Other than Him, nothing existed which since has been. Darkness there was; for this universe was enveloped with darkness, and was indistinguishable waters; but that mass, which was covered by the husk, was at length produced by the power of contemplation. First desire was formed in his mind; and that became the original productive seed; which the wise, recognizing it by the intellect in their hearts, distinguish as the bond of nonentity with entity.

DID the luminous ray of these creative acts expand in the middle, or above, or below? That productive energy became providence (or sentient souls), and matter (or the elements); Nature, who is sustained within, was inferior; and he who sustains was above.

WHO knows exactly, and who shall in this world declare, whence and why this creation took place? The gods are subsequent to the production of this world; then who can know whence it proceeded, or whence this varied world arose, or whether it upholds itself or not? He who in the highest heaven is the ruler of this universe, — he knows, or does not know.

### HYMN TO VARUNA

LET me not yet, O Varuna, enter into the house of clay; have mercy, almighty, have mercy.

If I go along trembling, like a cloud driven by the wind, have mercy, almighty, have mercy!

Through want of strength, thou strong and bright god, have I gone to the wrong shore; have mercy, almighty, have mercy!

Thirst came upon the worshipper, though he stood in the midst of the waters; have mercy, almighty, have mercy!

Whenever we men, O Varuna, commit an offence before the heavenly host; whenever we break thy law through thoughtlessness; have mercy, almighty, have mercy!

### The Beginning

IN the beginning there arose the Source of golden light. He was the only born lord of all that is. He established the earth, and this sky. Who is the God to whom we shall offer our sacrifice?

HE who gives life. He who gives strength; whose blessing all the bright gods desire; whose shadow is immortality, whose shadow is death. Who is the God to whom we shall offer our sacrifice?

HE who through his power is the only king of the breathing and awakening world. He who governs all, man and beast. Who is the god to whom we shall offer our sacrifice?

HE whose power these snowy mountains, whose power the sea proclaims, with the distant river. He whose these regions are, as it were his two arms. Who is the god to whom we shall offer our sacrifice?

HE through whom the sky is bright and the earth firm. He through whom heaven was stablished; nay, the highest heaven. He who measured out the light in the air. Who is the god to whom we shall offer our sacrifice?

HE to whom heaven and earth, standing firm by his will, look up, trembling inwardly. He over whom the rising sun shines forth. Who is the god to whom we shall offer our sacrifice?

WHEREVER the mighty water-clouds went, where they placed the seed and lit the fire, thence arose he who is the only life of the bright gods. Who is the god to whom we shall offer our sacrifice?

HE who by his might looked even over the water-clouds, the clouds which gave strength and lit the sacrifice; he who is God above all gods. Who is the god to whom we shall offer our sacrifice?

MAY he not destroy us, — he the creator of the earth, — or he, the righteous, who created heaven; he who also created the bright and mighty waters. Who is the god to whom we shall offer our sacrifices?

## HYMN TO INDRA

LET no one, not even those who worship thee, delay thee far from us! Even from afar come to our feast! Or, if thou art here, listen to us!

For these who here make prayers for thee, sit together near the libation, like flies round the honey. The worshippers, anxious for wealth, have placed their desire upon Indra, as we put our foot upon a chariot.

Desirous of riches, I call him who holds the thunderbolt with his arm, and who is a good giver, like as a son calls his father.

These libations of Soma, mixed with milk, have been prepared for Indra; thou, armed with the thunderbolt, come with the steeds to drink of them for thy delight; come to the house!

May he hear us, for he has ears to hear. He is asked for riches; will he despise our prayers? He could soon give hundreds and thousands; — no one could check him if he wishes to give.

Make for the sacred gods a hymn that is not small, that is well set and beautiful! Many snares pass by him who abides with Indra through his sacrifice.

What mortal dares to attack him who is rich in thee? Through faith in thee, O mighty, the strong acquires spoil in the days of battle.

Thou art well known as the benefactor of every one, whatever battles there be. Every one of these kings of the earth implores thy name when wishing for help.

If I were lord of as much as thou, I should support the sacred bard, thou scatterer of wealth, I should not abandon him to misery.

I should award wealth day by day to him who magnifies; I should award it to whosoever it be.

We have no other friend but thee, no other happiness, no other father, O mighty!

We call for thee, O hero, like cows that have not been milked; we praise thee as ruler of all that moves, O Indra, as ruler of all that is immovable.

There is no one like thee on heaven and earth; he is not born, and will not be born. O mighty Indra, we call upon thee as we go fighting for cows and horses.

## Hymn to the Dawn

WITH fortune shine forth upon us, O Dawn,
　　daughter of Heaven,
With mighty splendour, O lustrous one, with
　　wealth, bounteous goddess.

Horse-bringing, kine-bringing, well finding all
　　things, they ofttimes have sped to shine.
Send forth blessings to me, O Dawn; stir up the
　　bounty of the generous.

Maiden-like, gracious, Dawn cometh shewing kindness,
Bestirring all beings; foot-faring things go forth;
　　she maketh birds to fly up.

She who breaketh up the gathering and sendeth
　　forth men in business, the dewy one, brooketh not a resting place.
The birds at thy dawning, O mighty one, fly
　　forth and stay not still.

She hath ridden from afar, from the rising place
of the Sun;
This blessed Dawn cometh forth with an hundred
cars toward men.

The whole world boweth for sight of her; gracious,
she maketh light.
May Dawn, Heaven's bounteous daughter, shine
away feud and enmities!

O Dawn, beam thou with bright beam, daughter
of Heaven.
Bringing us abundant fortune, shining forth on
holy rites.

For the breath, the life of every being is with thee,
when thou shinest forth, O gracious one;
Lustrous, marvellous of bounty, do thou with thy
mighty ear hearken to our call.

O Dawn, do thou win thee power that is marvellous among mankind;
Bring therewith the righteous to the sacrifices,
the guides who sing of thee.

Bring thou all the gods to drink the Soma from
the sky, O Dawn;
Bestow on us praiseworthy possession of kine and
horses, O Dawn, gain with goodly manhood.

### Funeral Rites

As soon as he enters that life, he will become the servant of the gods.

May the eye go to the sun, the breath to the wind; go to the sky and the earth, as is right, or go to the waters, if it is good for thee there; rest in the plants.

The unborn part, warm it with thy warmth, may thy heat warm it and thy flame! O Gatavedas, carry him in thy kindliest shape to the world of those who have done well.

O Agni, send him back to Pitris, he who comes sacrificed with offering to thee! When clothed with life, may what remains come back, may he be joined with a body, O Gatavedas!

Whatever the black bird injured, the ant, the snake, or a wild beast, may Agni make that whole from all mischief, and Soma who has entered into the Brahmans!

Creep close to the mother, that earth there, the broad, the all-embracing, the blissful! She is like a maiden, soft like wool to the pious; may she guard thee from the lap of Nirriti (destruction).

O Earth, open wide, do not press him, be kind in admitting and in embracing him! Cover him, O Earth, as a mother covers her son with her cloth.

May the opened earth stand firm, and may a thousand supports stand near; may these dwellings be running with ghrita-offerings, and may there always be safety for him there!

## Time

Time carries us forward, a steed with seven rays, a thousand eyes, undecaying, full of fecundity. On him intelligent sages mount; his wheels are all the worlds.

Thus time moves on seven wheels; he has seven naves; immortality is his axle.

It is he who drew forth the worlds and encircled them. Being the father, he became their son. There is no other power superior to him.

Time generated the sky and these earths. Set in motion by Time, the past and the future subsist.

## The Gamester

The gamester comes to the assembly glowing in body and inquiring, "Shall I win?" The dice inflame his desire, making over his winnings to his opponent.

Deceitful, vexatious, delighting to torment, the dice dispense transient gifts, and again ruin the winner; they are covered with honey but destroy the gambler.

Their troop of fifty-three disports itself (disposing men's destinies) like the god Savitri whose ordinances never fail. They bow not before the wrath even of the fiercest. The king himself makes obeisance to them. They roll downward. They bound upward. Having no hands, they overcome him who has. These celestial coals when thrown on the dice-board scorch the heart though cold themselves.

The destitute wife of the gambler is distressed and so too is the mother of a son who goes she knows not whither. In debt and seeking after money, the gambler approaches with trepidation the houses of other people at night.

# BRĀHMANIC WISDOM

### Humility Unites Man with God

THERE is nothing stronger than an humble man, because an humble man, renouncing self, yields to God.

BEAUTIFUL are the words of the prayer: "Come and dwell in us." All is comprised in these words. Man has all that he requires if God comes to dwell in him. So that God may dwell in us, we must do only one thing: diminish ourselves in order to give place to God. As soon as man has diminished himself, God enters and dwells in him. Therefore in order to have all that is needful to him, man must first humble himself.

THE more deeply man penetrates into self, and the more insignificant he appears to himself, the higher he rises towards God.

HE who worships the All-Highest pride flees from his heart even as the light of a camp fire before the rays of the sun. He whose heart is pure and in whom there is no pride, he who is humble, constant and simple, who looks upon every creature as upon his friend and loves every soul as his own, he who treats every creature with equal tenderness and love, he who would do good and has abandoned vanity — in his heart dwelleth the lord of life.

EVEN as the earth is adorned with beautiful plants which she brings forth, even so is he adorned in whose soul dwelleth the Lord of life.

## DELUSION OF PERSONALITY

MANY imagine that if we eliminate personality and the love of it out of our life nothing will remain. They imagine that there is no life without personality. But this seems so only to people who have never experienced the joys of self-renunciation. Eliminate personality from life, renounce it and that will remain which forms the substance of life — love which yields positive happiness.

THE more man recognizes his spiritual "I," and the more he renounces his material personality, the more truly he understands himself.

## APPRECIATION OF GOOD THOUGHTS

APPRECIATE good thoughts, your own and those of others, as soon as you recognize them. Nothing will aid you as much as good thoughts in the accomplishment of the true task of your life.

Be master of your thoughts if you would attain your purpose. Fix the glance of your soul upon that one pure light which is free from passions.

### Control of Thoughts

WHEN misfortunes befall you know that they are not due to what you have done, but to what you have thought.

IF we cannot restrain ourselves from committing a deed which we know is evil, it is due to the fact only that we first permitted ourselves to think of this evil act and failed to restrain our thoughts.

STRIVE not to think of the things which you believe to be evil.

MORE injurious than evil acts are those thoughts which lead to evil acts. An evil act need not be repeated and it can be repented. But evil thoughts give birth to evil deeds. An evil act points the path to other evil acts. Evil thoughts drag you along upon the path to evil deeds.

FRUIT is born of a seed. Even so deeds are born of thoughts. Even as evil fruit is born of evil seed, so evil acts are born of evil thoughts. As a farmer separates good and true seed from the seed of weeds, and selects from among the good seed the choicest and guards and sorts it; even so a prudent man treats his thoughts; he repels vain and foolish thoughts, and preserves the good thoughts, cherishing and assorting them. If you do not repel evil thoughts, nor cherish good thoughts, you can not avoid evil acts. Good deeds come from good thoughts only. Cherish good thoughts, searching for them in books of wisdom, in sensible conversations and above all in your inner self.

## DARKENING SHADOWS

SO that a lamp may give steady light it must be placed where it is protected from the wind. But if a lamp is in a windy place, the light will flicker and cast strange and dark shadows. Even so uncontrolled, foolish and ill-assorted thoughts cast strange and dark shadows upon the soul of man.

WHEN the light of your spiritual life is being extinguished, the dark shadows of your bodily desires fall across your path,— beware of these dreadful shadows: the light of your spirit can not dissipate their darkness until you expel the desires of the body from your soul.

## HAPPINESS OF SPIRITUAL LIFE

JUST as a candle can not burn without a fire, man can not live without a spiritual life. The spirit dwells in all men, but not all men are aware of this.

HAPPY is the life of him who knows this, and unhappy his life who does not know it.

## The Eternal Principle

YOUR shadows live and vanish. That which is eternal in you, that which has reason, does not belong to the evanescent life. This eternal principle is within you, transport yourself into it, and it will reveal unto you that which is life and all that which is true and all that which you need know.

# INTRODUCTION

### TO THE MAHA-BHARATA AND RAMAYANA

ANCIENT INDIA, like ancient Greece, boasts of two great Epics. The Maha-Bharata, based on the legends and traditions of a great historical war, is the Iliad of India. The Ramayana, describing the wanderings and adventures of a prince banished from his country, has so far something in common with the Odyssey.

The scene of the Maha-Bharata is the ancient kingdom of the Kurus, which flourished along the upper course of the Ganges; and the historical fact on which the Epic is based is a great war which took place between the Kurus and a neighbouring tribe, the Panchalas, in the thirteenth or fourteenth century before Christ.

According to the Epic, Pandu and Dhrita-rashtra, who was born blind, were brothers. Pandu died early, and Dhrita-rashtra became king of the Kurus, and brought up the five sons of Pandu along with his hundred sons.

Yudhishthir, the eldest son of Pandu, was a man of truth and piety; Bhima, the second, was a stalwart fighter; and Arjun, the third son, distinguished himself above all the other princes in arms. The two youngest brothers, Nakula and

Sahadeva, were twins. Duryodhan was the eldest son of Dhrita-rashtra and was jealous of his cousins, the sons of Pandu. A tournament was held, and in the course of the day a warrior named Karna, of unknown origin, appeared on the scene and proved himself a worthy rival of Arjun. The rivalry between Arjun and Karna is the leading thought of the Epic, as the rivalry between Achilles and Hector is the leading thought of the Iliad.

It is only necessary to add that the sons of Pandu, as well as Karna, were, like the heroes of Homer, god-born chiefs. Some god inspired the birth of each. Yudhishthir was the son of Dharma, or Virtue, Bhima of Vayu or Wind, Arjun of Indra or Rain-god, the two youngest were the sons of the Aswin twins and Karna was the son of Surya the Sun, but was believed by himself and by all others to be the son of a simple chariot-driver.

The Ramayana, like the Maha-Bharata, is a growth of centuries, but the main story is more distinctly the creation of one mind. Among the many cultured races that flourished in Northern India about a thousand years before Christ, the Kosalas of Oudh and the Videhas of North Behar were perhaps the most cultured. Their monarchs were famed for their learning as well as for their prowess. Their priests distinguished themselves by founding schools of learning, which were known all over India. Their sacrifices and gifts to the learned drew together the most renowned men of the age from distant regions. Their celebrated Universities (Parishads) were frequented by students from surrounding countries. Their compilations of the old Vedic Hymns were used in various parts of India. Their elaborate Brahmanas or Commentaries on the Vedas were handed down from generation to generation by priestly families. Their researches into the mysteries of the Soul, and into the nature of the One Universal Soul which pervades the creation, are still preserved in the ancient Upanishads, and are among the most valuable heritages which have been left to us by the ancients. And their researches and discoveries in science and philosophy gave them the foremost place among the gifted races of ancient India.

It would appear that the flourishing period of the Kosalas and the Videhas had already passed away and the traditions of their prowess and learning had become a revered memory in India, when the poet composed the great Epic which perpetuates their fame. Distance of time lent a higher lustre to the achievements of these gifted races and the age in which they flourished appeared to their descendants as the Golden Age of India. To the imagination of the poet, the age of the Kosalas and Videhas was associated with all that is great and glorious, all that is righteous and true. His description of Ayodhya, the capital town of Kosalas, is a description of an ideal seat of righteousness. Dasa-ratha, the king of the Kosalas, is an ideal king, labouring for the good of a loyal people. Rama, the eldest son of Dasaratha and the hero of the Epic, is an ideal prince, brave and accomplished, devoted to his duty, unfaltering in his truth. The king of the Videhas, Janak, is a monarch and a saint. Sita, the daughter of Janak and the heroine of the Epic, is the ideal of a faithful woman and a devoted wife. A pious reverence for the past pervades the great Epic; a lofty admiration of what is true and ennobling in the human character sanctifies the work; and delineations of the domestic life and the domestic virtues of the ancient Hindus, rich in hearts of and pathos, endear the picture to the tenderness the people of India to the present day.

It is probable that the first connected narrative of this Epic was composed within a few centuries after the glorious age of the Kosalas and the Videhas. But the work became so popular that it grew with age. It grew,— not like the Maha-Bharata by the incorporation of new episodes, tales and traditions,— but by fresh descriptions of the same scenes and incidents. Generations of poets were never tired of adding to the description of scenes which were dear to the Hindu, and patient Hindu listeners were never tired of listening to such repetitions. The virtues of Rama and the faithfulness of Sita were described again and again in added lines and cantos. The grief of the old monarch at the banishment of the prince, and the sorrows of the mother at parting from her son, were depicted by succeeding versifiers in fresh verses. The loving devotion of Rama's brothers, the sanctity of saints, and the peacefulness of the hermitages visited by Rama, were described with endless reiteration. The long account of the grief of Rama at the loss of his wife, and stories of unending battles waged for her recovery, occupied generations of busy interpolators.

The foregoing account of the genesis and growth of 'the Ramayana will indicate in what respects it resembles the Maha-Bharata, and in what respects the two Indian Epics differ from each other. The Maha-Bharata grew out of the legends and traditions of a great historical war between the Kurus and the Panchalas; the Ramayana grew out of the recollections of the golden age of the Kosalas and the Videhas. The characters of the Maha-Bharata are characters of flesh and blood, with the virtues and crimes of great actors in the historic world; the characters of the Ramayana are more often the ideals of manly devotion to truth, and of womanly faithfulness and love in domestic life. The poet of the Maha-Bharata relies on the real or supposed incidents of a war handed down from generation to generation in songs and ballads, and weaves them into an immortal work of art; the poet of the Ramayana conjures up the memories of a golden age, constructs lofty ideals of piety and faith, and describes with infinite pathos domestic scenes and domestic affections which endear the work to modern Hindus. As a heroic poem the Maha-Bharata stands on a higher level; as a poem delineating the softer emotions of our everyday life the Ramayana sends its roots deeper into the hearts and minds of the millions in India.

And yet, without rivalling the heroic grandeur of the Maha-Bharata, the Ramayana is immeasurably superior in its delineation of these softer and perhaps deeper emotions which enter into our everyday life, and hold the world together. And these descriptions, essentially of Hindu life, are yet so true to nature that they apply to all races and nations.

There is something indescribably touching and tender in the description of the love of Rama for his subjects and the loyalty of his people towards Rama,— that loyalty which has ever been a part of the Hindu character in every age.

Deeper than this was Rama's duty towards his father and his father's fondness for Rama; and the portion of the Epic which narrates the dark scheme by which the prince was at last torn from the heart and home of his dying father is one of the most powerful and pathetic passages in Indian literature. The stepmother of Rama, won by the virtues and the kindliness of the prince, regards his proposed coronation with pride and pleasure, but her old nurse creeps into her confidence like a creeping serpent, and envenoms her heart with the poison of her own wickedness. She arouses the slumbering jealousy of a woman and awakens the alarms of a mother.

The nurse's dark insinuations work on the mind of the queen till she becomes a desperate woman, resolved to maintain her own influence on her husband, and to see her own son on the throne. The determination of the young queen tells with terrible effect on the weakness and vacillation of a feeble old monarch, and Rama is banished at last. And the scene closes with a pathetic story in which the monarch recounts his misdeed of past years, accepts his present suffering as the fruit of that misdeed, and dies in agony for his banished son.

The inner workings of the human heart and of human motives, the dark intrigue of a scheming dependent, the awakening jealousy and alarm of a wife and a mother, the determination of a woman and an imperious queen, and the feebleness and despair and death of a fond old father and husband, have never been more vividly described. Shakespeare himself has not depicted the workings of stormy passions in the human heart more graphically or more vividly, with greater truth or with more terrible power.

It is truth and power in the depicting of such scenes, and not in the delineation of warriors and warlike incidents, that the Ramayana excels. It is in the delineation of domestic incidents, domestic affections and domestic jealousies, which are appreciated by the prince and the peasant alike, that the Ramayana bases its appeal to the hearts of the million in India. And beyond all this, the righteous devotion of Rama, and the faithfulness and womanly love of Sita, run like two threads of gold through the whole fabric of the Epic, and ennoble and sanctify the work in the eyes of Hindus.

Rama and Sita are the Hindu ideals of a Perfect Man and a Perfect Woman; their truth under trials and temptations, their endurance under privations, and their devotion to duty under all vicissitudes of fortune, form the Hindu ideal of a Perfect Life. In this respect the Ramayana gives us a true picture of Hindu faith and righteous life as Dante's "Divine Comedy" gives us a picture of the faith and belief of the Middle Ages in Europe. Our own ideals in the present day may not be the ideals of the tenth century before Christ or the fourteenth century after Christ; but mankind will not willingly let die those great creations of the past which shadow forth the ideals and beliefs of interesting periods in the progress of human civilisation.

Sorrow and suffering, trial and endurance, are a part of the Hindu ideal of a Perfect Life of righteousness. Rama suffers for fourteen years in exile, and is chastened by privations and misfortunes, before he ascends the throne of his father. In a humble way this course of training was passed through by every pious Hindu of the ancient times. Every Aryan boy in India was taken away from his parents at an early age, and lived the hard life of an anchorite under his teacher for twelve or twenty-four or thirty-six years, before he entered the married life and settled down as a householder. Every Aryan boy assumed the rough garment and the staff and girdle of a student, lived as a mendicant and begged his food from door to door, attended on his preceptor as a menial, and thus trained himself in endurance and suffering as well as in the traditional learning of the age, before he became a householder. The pious Hindu saw in Rama's life the ideal of a true Hindu life, the success and the triumph which follow upon endurance and faith and devotion to duty. It is the truth and endurance of Rama under sufferings and privations which impart the deepest lessons to the Hindu character, and is the highest ideal of a Hindu righteous life. The ancient ideal may seem to us far-fetched in these days, but we can never fully comprehend the great moral Epic of the Hindus unless we endeavour to study fully and clearly its relations to old Hindu ideas and old Hindu life.

And if trial and endurance are a part of a Hindu's ideal of a man's life, devotion and self-abnegation are still more essentially a part of his ideal of a woman's life. Sita holds a place in the hearts of women in India which no other creation of a poet's imagination holds among any other nation on earth. There is not a Hindu woman whose earliest and tenderest recollections do not cling round the story of Sita's sufferings and Sita's faithfulness, told in the nursery, taught in the family circle, remembered and cherished through life. Sita's adventures in a desolate forest and in a hostile prison only represent in an exaggerated form the humbler trials of a woman's life; and Sita's endurance and faithfulness teach her devotion to duty in all trials and troubles of life.

The ideal of life was joy and beauty and gladness in ancient Greece; the ideal of life was piety and endurance and devotion in ancient India. The tale of Helen was a tale of womanly beauty and loveliness which charmed the western world. The tale of Sita was a tale of womanly faith and self-abnegation which charmed and fascinated the Hindu world. Repeated trials bring out in brighter relief the unfaltering truth of Sita's character; she goes to a second banishment in the woods with the same trust and devotion to her lord as before, and she returns once more, and sinks into the bosom of her Mother Earth, true in death as she had been true in life. The creative imagination of the Hindus has conceived no loftier and holier character than Sita: the literature of the world has not produced a higher ideal of womanly love, womanly truth, and womanly devotion.

The modern reader will now comprehend why India produced, and has preserved for well-nigh three thousand years, two Epics instead of one national Epic. No work of the imagination abides long unless it is animated by some sparks of imperishable truth, unless it truly embodies some portion of our human feelings, human faith and human life. The Maha-Bharata depicts the political life of ancient India, with all its valour and heroism, ambition and lofty chivalry. The Ramayana embodies the domestic and religious life of ancient India, with all its tenderness and sweetness, its endurance and devotion. The one picture without the other were incomplete, and we should know but little of the ancient Hindus if we did not comprehend their inner life and faith as well as their political life and warlike virtues. The two together give us a true and graphic picture of ancient Indian life and civilisation; and no nation on earth has preserved a more faithful picture of its glorious past.

# SELECTIONS FROM THE MAHÁ–BHÁRATA

### The Desires

THE Brahman said: "Look how creatures of the highest, midway and lowest degrees are everywhere here enmeshed in grief because of their works. Even this my soul here is not mine; or rather, the whole earth is mine, and as it is mine, so it belongs likewise to others; thus I think, and abide undisturbed. Having gained this vision, I rejoice not and grieve not. As in the great ocean one piece of wood meets another, and after meeting they again part from one another, such is the meeting of creatures."

### Earthly Affection

THUS it is with children and children's children, with friends and kinsmen; it is not well to have love for them, for parting from them is inevitable. Come hither from the dark and again gone back into the dark, another knows not thee, and thou knowest not him; who then art thou, and what is anything, that thou lamentest for it? From the stress of desire arises grief, from the stress of grief arises pleasure, and from pleasure again arises grief, and again grief. The immediate issue of pleasure is grief, the immediate issue of grief is pleasure; pleasure and grief among men roll round like a wheel. When thou hast passed from pleasure into grief, thou wilt thence pass once more into pleasure; men cannot for ever have grief, nor for ever have pleasure.

THE body is the seat alike of grief and of pleasure. Life also arises together with this body; both wax together, and both together decay. Men are held by the manifold snares of the desires in the world of sense, and they fall away without winning to thir end, like dykes of sand in water.

## LOVE OF MATERIAL POSSESSIONS

LIKE sesame-grains for their oil, all things are ground out in the mill-wheel of creation by the oil-grinders, to wit, the taints arising from ignorance, which fasten upon them. The husband gathers to himself evil works on account of his wife; but he alone is therefore afflicted with taints, which cling to man alike in the world beyond and in this. All men are attached to children, wives, and kin; they sink down in the slimy sea of sorrows, like age-worn forest-elephants.

ON the loss of children, on the loss of substance or of friends and kinsmen, men suffer exceeding anguish, like the fire of a burning forest. This whole world depends upon Fate in pleasure and pain, in birth and unborn being. Whether a man have friends or not, whether he have foes or allies, whether he be wise or void of wisdom, he gets his happiness through Fate.

### Waywardness of Fortune

FRIENDS suffice not to make one happy, nor foes to make one unhappy; wisdom suffices not to make one wealthy, wealth suffices not to make happy. Prudence is not enough to attain wealth, foolishness hinders not success; the wise man, not the fool, understands this course of the world's way. Fortune follows whomsoever she meets, the understanding and bold, the silly and cowardly, the dull and the wise, the weakly and the strong. The cow belongs to the calf, to the herdsman, to the master, and to the thief; to him who drinks her milk the cow verily belongs. The most foolish in the world and the most prudent easily win success; but he who stands midway between them is afflicted.

### Pleasure and Grief

PLEASURE, when it is of the spirit of sloth, ends in grief; grief, when it is of the spirit of energy, leads to pleasure; prosperity and happiness dwell with the man of energy, not with the slothful. But whether it be pleasure or pain, sweet or bitter, a man should bear with what befalls, as it befalls, unconquered of spirit. A thousand motives of sorrow and a hundred motives of fear fall daily upon the erring, but none upon the wise.

## Conquest of Sorrow

GRIEF touches not him who is understanding, who has won illumination, seeks for knowledge of scripture, and is free from envy, self-controlled and master of his senses. The wise man should hold fast to this illumination and keep watch over his thoughts; then he knows how the world arises and dissolves, and no grief can touch him. Whatsoever be the cause whence may arise a grief or an affliction or a sorrow or a labour of spirit, a man should put away that from which these may spring, even though it were a limb of his own body. Whenever any work is done from a spirit of selfishness, in the issue it becomes a source of grief. Whatever desires are cast out, their place is filled up by happiness; but the man who runs after desires falls into destruction after his desires.

## Happiness

ALL happiness that may come from fulfilment of wishes in the world, and all the exceeding bliss that there may be in heaven, do not together weigh the sixteenth part of the happiness that consists in the destruction of desire. On the head of each man, be he wise or foolish or valiant, comes every good and evil work that has been done by him in former incarnation, according to the manner of its doing. Thus truly all these sweets and bitternesses, sorrows and joys in souls roll round and round.

### Freedom from Desires

HOLDING fast to this illumination, the good man sits in peace. He should guard himself from all desires; he should cast desires behind him. Wrath is the name of him who stirs in the heart, who when strengthened is as death dwelling in the spirit; abiding in the bodies of embodied beings, thus is he named by the wise.

WHEN a man has drawn inwards the desires, from all sides, as the tortoise gathers in its limbs, he shall behold the light of the Self as his Self in himself. When one fears none and none fear him, when he desires no longer and hates no longer, he passes into Brahma. When he surrenders alike the true and the untrue, sorrow and joy, fear and courage, when he leaves behind him the sweet and the bitter, he will live in peace of soul. When he in wisdom does no kind of hurt to any creatures, either in work or in thought or in words, he passes into Brahma. Desire is a sickness that is hard for the foolish to abandon, which ages not with man's ageing, which only ends with life itself; blessed is he who frees himself from it!

## In Search of True Values

By death the world is afflicted, by age it is held in bar, and the nights are the Unfailing ones that are ever coming and going. When I know that death cannot halt, what can I expect from walking in a cover of lore? If life grows ever shorter as night after night passes by, then the man of understanding may likewise find his days barren. Who could feel joy where he is like a fish in shallow water? Before he sees his desires fulfilled, death falls upon man. Death will seize upon him, while he is gathering flowers and his thought is turned elsewhere, even as a she-wolf seizes upon a lamb, and hastens away with his prey.

This very day do what is to thy best profit; let not this hour pass over thy head; for death carries away a man ere yet his tasks are fulfilled. Rather should one do to-day the work of the morrow rather in the forenoon the work of the afternoon; for death waits not, whether one has brought to an end his labour or not. Yea, who knows whose hour of death will be to-day. Let even the youth accustom himself to do his duty, for life is frail. Fulfilled duty brings honour on earth and bliss in the world beyond.

Possessed by delusion a man toils for wife and child; but whether he have fulfilled his purpose or not, he must surrender the enjoyment thereof.

When one is blessed with children and flocks, and his heart is clinging unto them, death carries him away, as a tiger a sleeping deer. While he is still gathering, and while his desires are still unfulfilled, death carries him away, as a tiger an ox. While one is busied in strivings and gratifications, thinking "this is done, this must be done, and this other matter is half done," death overcomes him.

BE he weak or strong, a valiant man or a coward, foolish or prudent, death carries him away ere he has reached the goal of all his wishes. As death and age, sickness and sorrow, arising from many causes, attach to the body, how canst thou remain composed? Death and age pursue all that are born for their destruction; to these two all creatures, unmoving and moving alike, are subject. The town-dweller's love of wife is a door of death, but the forest is a meeting-place of the gods, says holy writ. The town-dweller's love of wife is a fettering snare; the good break it and escape, the bad break it not. He who does no hurt to creatures either in thought or in word or by his body, gets likewise no hurt from the living things which take away life and possessions.

WITHOUT the Truth no man can ever defeat the assailing host of Death; untruth must be renounced, for in truth is the seat of immortality. Therefore he who walks under the vows of truth, and devotes himself to union with truth, and has a true scripture and is constantly self-controlled, overcomes death by the truth. Alike the need to die no more and the need to die have their foundation in bodily life. The need to die arises from delusion; from truth arises the need to die no more.

I, WHO do hurt to none, who long for truth, who have cast away desire and wrath, and am indifferent and content in pleasure and pain, shall become free from death, like one of the immortals. Rejoicing in peace as my sacrifice, self-controlled, abiding in the worship of Brahma, a saint offering the sacrifice of word, thought, and deed, I shall pass away by the sun's northern road. How should one such as I bring a bloody sacrifice of beasts? — the wise man bring living offerings bearing temporal fruit, like a devil? He who has utterly suppressed words and thoughts for ever, who practises mortification, self-denial, and truth, verily wins the universe.

No eye is peer to knowledge, no mortification to truth; no sorrow is equal to passion, no happiness to self-denial. Born in my Self by my self, established in myself, albeit without offspring, I shall live in my Self alone; offspring cannot save me. No wealth is so precious for a Brahman as concord, indifference, truthfulness, goodness, firmness, harmlessness, uprightness, and gradual withdrawing from works in their order. What should avail thee wealth, or kindred, or wives, O Brahman, since thou must die? Seek thou the Self, which is lodged in its covert. Whither have thy forefathers and thy father gone?

## Savitri's Love
### *From the Maha-Bharata*

Now, there was a king in India, whose name was Aswapati (As-wa-pah-tee), and his people loved him, for he gave help to all in need, and he served the shining gods in prayer and sacrifice.

But he had no son or daughter in whom his name and line could live on, when the time came for him to die, and his heart was grieved, and he fasted oft, and said hymns to the shining gods, and burned offerings on their holy altar, and hoped they would grant him the gift he asked. When sixteen years had thus passed, his prayer was heard. In the red fire of the altar he beheld a lady of fair look and ways, and she said to him:

"Thy faith hath pleased me, O Raja, and if thou wilt say thy desire, it shall be given thee."

"Goddess," replied the king, "my wish is to have a child to live after me."

"The Lord of heaven," she said, "will grant thee what thou hast prayed."

She was gone and the Raja saw only the red flame.

A babe was born — a girl, with bright eyes, bright like the lotus lily, as the Indian people say — and she was the glory of her mother and father. She grew to be so sweet a maid that her father made sure that kings would come from far and near to seek her as a wife. But none came, for she — the lotus-eyed — had a soul that seemed too great for even kings, and her serious ways and speech kept men in awe.

Now, one day, this maid of grace — Savitri (Sah-vee-tree) by name — had knelt at the altar of Agni, god of the red flame, and had laid there an offering of cakes and drink. Then she took up a bunch of flowers in the holy place, and came and gave them to her sire, Aswapati. He gazed upon her with tender eyes and said:

"Daughter, it is time you should be wed after the manner of high-born ladies, lest folk should think that I am at fault in not choosing a husband for you. And since no man comes to pay suit to you I pray you go where you will and choose for yourself."

So she bowed herself before her sire, and took her leave, and rode in a splendid car along with elders and wise men, whom the king had told to go with her up and down the land. The car passed through forests and along the streets of great towns, and among the hamlets of the hills, and wherever she went the princess gave alms to the poor and greetings to the high and low, and the people blessed her.

At last she came back and the Raja was on his throne, and the wise man, Narad, sat at his side.

"Father," she said, "I have done as you bade,

and I have found my choice. It is the Prince Satyavan. Prince he is, yet he dwells not in a royal house."

"Wherefore?" asked the Raja.

"He has no kingdom, and lives in a cottage in the woods with his father and mother. A noble pair are they, but sad is their lot. The old man is blind, and he and his queen have had their home many years, ever since their son was a babe, in this jungle, for enemies drove them from their kingdom, and took from the king his rightful throne. My prince is noble, and his name shows what he is, for at his birth the Brahmans called him Truth-lover. Gay and strong is he, and a rider of horses, and his hand has a gift for painting horses in pictures that are a wonder to see."

"What think you?" asked the king of Narad, the wise.

"Alas!" answered Narad, "ill has she chosen. The old king indeed is a just man, and the Prince Satyavan is a noble youth, but there is a dark fate that waits for him, for it has been shown to me by the shining gods that in a year from this very day he shall die."

"Hear you that, my daughter?" cried the king. "O choose some other, choose some other, for the Lord of Death, even Yama, will come in a year and claim your husband for his own. Choose some other."

"I can choose none other, father dear," said

the maid. "To Satyavan alone is my heart given, and though Death will take him in a year, yet him only will I wed."

"Let it be so, child," sighed the Raja. "Strange will your bridal be. You will have your home in the wilderness, and in twelve months be left a mourner."

The king and his courtiers and priests set forth to the woods, carrying with them much treasure, and they found the blind old king seated on a grass mat beside a sal tree.

"Be seated, sir!" said the blind Raja, when he knew that a king had come to see him.

So Aswapati sat on the grass mat, and the blind king offered him water from a jar, for he was poor, and had neither wine nor silver cups. And the two kings agreed upon the marriage, and soon the prince and the maid were wed in the forest, and when she was made lady of the little cot among the trees of the jungle, her sire kissed her with many tears, and her friends said farewells, and they departed. As soon as they were gone, she took off her jewels and sparkling dress, and she put on a plain robe made of bark of trees, and a cloak of yellow cloth. Her queenhood was not in her jewels or her dress, but in her kind soul and the sweet service she did to the blind old king and his wife, and in the love she bore to the prince of her choice.

So passed the happy year, and only four days more would go by ere the Shadow of Death would glide into the forest kingdom of her lord, and take him from her arms. For three days she fasted and she had no sleep, and her heart was in pain at the dread of that which was to come. But Satyavan, the noble prince, knew naught of the fate that waited for his life.

On the morning of the last day rose Satyavan, in blithe mood, and he took his woodsman's axe for felling trees, and said, smiling:

"Dear wife, I go forth to hew down trees, and at set of sun, I shall be home again."

Her heart smote her at the words, for she knew that the black-robed Yama would lay his thin hand upon her love and take him hence.

"I will go with you this day," she said.

"Nay," he cried, "the ground is rough for your feet, and the way will be long, and you will be faint."

"Let me go, Satyavan," begged the princess in the robe of bark.

He said her nay no more, and they walked to the distant spot where grew the trees he meant to fell, and the wild fruit that she would gather in her basket.

The hour of noon had passed, and the dusk was creeping upon the great forest. The sound of the axe echoed in the grove. Basket in hand, Savitri plucked ripe berries from the shrubs, but often and often she paused and she looked at the wood-cutter, and she looked again. . . .

"Oh, wife," he called.

She ran to his side and set her basket down.

"My head, my head! A pang shoots sharp through my brain. Hot is my blood. I must lie down."

She sat beneath a tree and laid his head upon her lap, and fanned his face. His eyes were closed, his pulse was slow, and now it was still.

The year had flown.

Before her stood a tall shadow that had the shape of a man, and its robe was black, and a red light was in its eyes, and a crown was on its head.

"Are you one of the holy gods?" she asked in a low voice.

"Lady," it said, "I am Yama, the Lord of Death, and I am come for the prince you love."

He lifted his hand, and in it was a cord, and he flung the cord, and lo! it caught the life of the prince in its noose, and drew it from his bosom, and Satyavan was dead, and Death turned its face towards the south, for the south (so the Indian fables tell) was its kingdom.

Dark was the jungle.

Strong was Death.

But the woman was brave.

She rose up and followed in the steps of Death.

Presently the black god, hearing her footsteps, turned and spoke:

"Go back. You have come far from home. Go back, and do those sad rites in which mourners show their sorrow for the dead."

"I must go," she replied, "where my husband

goes. That is my duty. The wise men say that to walk seven steps with another makes them friends. So let me walk more than seven steps with you. And the wise men also say that the best road to walk is that of right."

"Well have you convinced me," said the Lord of Death, "and in return for the good words, I promise that, except the soul of Satyavan, I will give you what you will."

"Then give me a gift for my prince's father, and let the eyes of the old king once more behold the light of day, and let his strength be as the strength of the sun."

"It shall be done," said Death; "but now you must turn back, for you have far to go; and my way leads only to Doom."

"I shall never be weary of the way that my husband goes. There is no sweeter fruit on earth than the company of those we love."

The black god smiled, for her words were good and precious.

"Once again, I will give you a gift, except the soul of Satyavan."

"Thanks again, O Death; and now I will ask that the kingdom of the old Raja shall be restored to him, so that he may have his land as well as his sight."

"Lady, it shall happen as you wish. And now go back. The forest is wide, and home is distant."

"Master of Death, hear me once more. What is the goodness of the good man? Is it kindness to all things in earth, air or sea? It is indeed, and even if the enemy seeks help, the good man will be ready to grant him aid."

"Fair is your saying, princess; and for these blessed words I will promise yet another boon. Speak."

"O Death, I would be mother to noble children, and teach them to walk in the steps of their dear father, Satyavan. Give me my prince."

Then Yama, King of Death, shook the cord that he held in his hand.

"Lady, your husband shall reign long years with you, and your sons shall reign after you."

The dark shade that wore the crown had floated into the gloom of the jungle.

With quick feet she ran. Breathless, she flew. And when she reached the tree under which the body of Satyavan lay, she knelt, she placed the head on her lap, she watched; and the eyes opened, and the lips said:

"I have slept a long time. Just as I was falling into slumber, I seemed to see a vision of a shadow that seized my very life in a magic noose, and bore it away I know not where."

"It was Yama, Lord of Death. But he is not here. Rise, Satyavan, for it is night, and we must go home."

"Ah!" he said, "now I call to mind that a sharp pang shot through my brow."

"To-morrow let us talk of what has happened to-day. Let us go."

"The night is dark. We could not find the path."

"Look!" she said, "some way off a fire has been burning to-day in the forest — the work of the blazing sun at mid-day, perhaps. I will fetch a brand, and we will wave it as we walk, so as to scare away the beasts of the jungle. Or, if you will, let us stay here till your pain is all gone."

"It has gone, Savitri. I am strong again. My father and mother will grieve at our absence."

As he thought of his blind father (ah! but was he blind now?) the prince's eyes filled with tears.

So he sprang to his feet, and brushed off the dry leaves that clung to his clothes.

"There is your basket of fruit," he cried.

"Fetch it to-morrow, Satyavan. We have enough to do to find our way in the dark. But I will carry the axe."

She carried the axe in her left hand, and her right arm was about his waist; and his left arm was about her neck; and so they wended their way through the jungle; nor did bear or tiger harm them.

The sky was becoming grey when they reached the hamlet where the old king and queen and their few companions lived. They heard voices crying eagerly. A shout arose when the prince and princess were seen.

"My children!" cried the king.

"Father!" exclaimed Satyavan. "How is this? You were able to see me?"

"My son, my eyes can see once more. I know not how the marvel came about, but I do know I can see my son. And you, dear Savitri, for the first time can I now look upon my faithful daughter!"

After he had held them for some moments, and gazed at them both with joy, he asked:

"And where have you been all the night? Tell me, Satyavan, what kept you so long?"

"Father," said Savitri, "he does not know all that took place in the night. Let me tell the tale."

So they sat down — king, queen, prince, princess, and their comrades and loyal friends, and the soft voice of Savitri told:

How they wandered in the forest;

How the curse had been foretold by Narad, the sage, and how it must be fulfilled at the end of the year;

How Satyavan died;

How Death came;

And how she had followed Death and what had been said.

Now, while the king and his friends thus listened, and their hearts were moved by the story, a great noise was heard in the forest. Along the glade they saw a crowd of people approach— soldiers, officers, citizens.

"News, good news!" the people cried. "The tyrant who took the throne by unjust means and cruel power has been overthrown. Come back to us, dear king. Blind though you are, you shall at least know that we gather round you in true service."

"Thanks be to the shining gods, my people," said the old king, "I can see you all; and I will go with you, and see my kingdom once again."

### The Five Princes

*From the Maha-Bharata*

FIVE princes, brothers, wandered in a forest. They were the sons of an Indian king. Now this king had two wives, Koontee and Madree, and the young men were sons to one or the other of the queens. The two sons of Madree were thus half-brothers to the three sons of Koontee.

A hard fate drove them from their home-land. For thirteen years they must not see their country. For thirteen years they must be exiles. They must hide from their foes.

A dread place was the wood where they hid. Tall trees put out their great arms and made a black shade. The thin-legged deer ran to and fro in the glades. Bears stole in and out of the bushes. Snakes lurked in nooks. Wild bees hummed. Birds of strange shape flew from tree to tree.

The five princes, two sons of Madree, three sons of Koontee, felt a deep thirst, and nowhere could they see the sweet shine of water.

Then Yudhisthira, who was more than a prince—

he was a king — said to his half-brother Nakula:
"O Nakula, son of Madree, climb yonder tree and look all ways, and see if water is near; look if any plants that grow in moist soil are in this jungle, for they will be a sign of water."

Then Nakula, who was the twin-brother to Sahadev, went up the tree as he was bid, and he looked this way and that, and he made a shout:

"Yes, I can see plants and leaves that live in the damp. And hark! I can hear the sharp call of the cranes."

Said the king:

"Make haste, Nakula. Take your arrow-case with you and fill it with water at the pool or spring where the cranes are, and bring your brothers a precious draught!"

So Nakula came down with speed, and he ran with his quiver in hand to the place where he had caught sight of the green plants. A smooth, clear pool was there, and on the edge of it he beheld cranes, birds with long legs and long necks; their tails feathery, their eyes eager and watchful; and a red tuft was on each head. The cranes snapped at worms, at small snakes, at frogs, at fish, and now and then tore up a weed from the pool.

But the prince had no care for cranes. He was all but mad with thirst. Down on his knees he fell. He leaned his head to the clear pool.

"Stay!" cried a voice. "Stay, young man! Drink naught till you have done as the law of this pool bids. None may drink here till he has made answer to the questions I ask. Answer first, and then fill your quiver."

Nakula paid no heed. He drank. The next moment he fell dead among the reeds that grew at the brink of the water.

The cranes waded in the pool. Wild bees hummed. Deer trotted through the jungle. The dead prince held the quiver in his hand; and his four brothers waited.

Finding that he did not return, the king said:

"Sahadev, we will not wait longer. I know not why your brother delays. Go and fetch water for us, for we are faint, and can scarce move. Follow the track your brother went."

When Sahadev reached the water he saw the dead youth, and his heart was sore troubled; yet was his thirst so great that he had no will to stay and weep over his lost one, and he knelt to drink.

"Halt," cried a loud voice. "Do not take one drop of this water until you have made reply to my questions, else it will mean death!"

The prince said not a word. He bent over the pool, and then rolled upon the earth dead.

Side by side lay the brothers — the twin sons of Madree the queen. And the bear of the woods crept among the bushes in search of berries, and the gleam of the tiger's eyes was bright in the jungle.

Two brothers dead; three brothers living; and dry were the mouths of the three.

Said the king:

"Have you strength, Arjuna, brother of mine, to go to the pool and fetch water? Your brother and I are weak with thirst. Oh, haste, Arjuna, haste!"

When Arjuna saw his two dead brothers he put his arrow to the bow and looked about for the foe that had slain them, so that he might slay the slayer. But he saw no living man. Then the thirst came so strong upon him that he must drink; so he stooped down.

"Beware," cried a voice. "Drink not until you have answered my questions. To drink now will be your doom."

"Who are you, vile man?" shouted Arjuna; and he shot one arrow this way among the reeds, and another among the trees; and he pulled out darts from his bundle, and flung them up, and north and south, and east and west; but he saw no man.

"Ha, ha, ha," laughed the voice. "You cannot strike me, prince. Answer, if you wish to live."

Arjuna knelt and was about to drink. He also fell dead.

"Alas!" sighed the king, "they come not back. What can have happened? Perhaps they are all too faint to walk. Will you, dear Bhima, go for drink?"

Then Bhima rose slowly and crept to the pool, and he was in great sorrow when he saw the three dead youths; but he was so parched that he could not stay to mourn.

"Drink not," said the voice. "Let not water touch your lips till you have given answer to my questions; else you will breathe your last!"

And Bhima also died.

Silent was the forest, except for the murmur of bees and the sounds of bird and beast; and the king sat in pain of thirst. At last he arose, and with slow steps he wended his way to the pool.

Loud was his wail when he saw the four dead men, and he glanced all round to see who it was that smote them, but he could discover no enemy. And then he bent towards the water where grew the lilies.

"Stay!" cried the voice. "Unless you answer my questions ere you drink, death will fall upon you; such is the law of this place. I, the old crane with the red crest, rule over the pool, and I dare you to drink."

"No crane," replied the king, "would have such power. You must be some bad genie. Show yourself!"

He saw the crane amid the reeds.

"King," said the bird, "I am indeed a genie. But hearken unto my warning. Drink not yet."

"Repeat your questions."

"How can a man become wise?"

"By learning the sacred texts of the hymns — the blessed Vedas."

"Who is he that is not rich, though he looks well and fair?"

"The man who has much and gives naught."

"What is heavier than the world and higher than the clouds."

"The love of father and mother."

"Whose eyes never close?"

"The fish's eyes."

"Which is the way to be happy?"

"To say the truth and be kind."

"How may a man be a true Brahman?"

"Not by saying texts from the holy scriptures; not by praying many prayers; but by just deeds and right life."

These and other questions did the king answer.

Then said the spirit of the pool:

"Well have you spoken. Drink."

Then said the spirit of the pool again:

"Well pleased am I with your speech, and now I give you a boon. You may name which you will of these dead men, and he whom you choose shall live."

There was silence. Said the king:

"I will choose Nakula, son of Madree."

"But he is only your half-brother. Will you not choose your own brother, Bhima, or your own brother, Arjuna? Did you not love them?"

"Yea, I loved them," said the king. "But I wish that Nakula should come back to life."

"Why?"

"Because he is the son of Madree, and I am the son of Koontee. Now, after the thirteen years of wandering, we shall return to our home, and the two queens will come forth to see us. Two only of the five brethren will they see. And if Madree sees that both are the sons of Koontee, and she learns that her twin sons are dead, then will her heart faint and be like to break. Therefore, O spirit, let us be just to the mother's heart, and let one son of each mother bring gladness to their eyes."

The crane was no more seen. But as it fled away its voice was heard saying softly:

"Noble-hearted prince! You have chosen Nakula before your own dearest brothers, and you wished to be just rather than snatch at what would best please your own soul. Therefore they all shall live!"

And the four brothers rose up.

BE master of thyself, if thou wilt be
Servant of Duty. Such as thou shalt see
Not self-subduing, do no deeds of good
In youth or age, in household or in wood.
But wise men know that virtue is best bliss,
And all by some one way may reach to this.
It needs not men should pass through orders four
To come to knowledge; — doing right is more
Than any learning; therefore sages say
Best and most excellent is Virtue's way.

THERE is naught better than to be
With noble souls in company;
There is naught better than to wend
With good friends faithful to the end.
This is the love whose fruit is sweet,
Therefore to bide within is meet.

THE constant virtues of the good are tenderness and love
To all that lives — in earth, air, sea — great, small — below, above;
Compassionate of heart, they keep a gentle thought for each,
Kind in their actions, mild in will, and pitiful of speech;
Who pitieth not, he hath not faith; full many an one so lives,
But when an enemy seeks help, a good man gladly gives.

IN paths of peace and virtue
Always the good remain;
And sorrow shall not stay with them,
Nor long access of pain;
At meeting or at parting
Joys to their bosom strike;
For good to good is friendly,
And virtue loves her like.

The great sun goes his journey
By their strong truth impelled;
By their pure lives and penances

Is earth itself upheld;
Of all which live and shall live
Upon its hills and fields,
True hearts are the protectors,
For virtue saves and shields.

Never are noble spirits
Poor while their like still live;
True love has gems to render,
And virtue wealth to give.
Never is lost or wasted
The goodness of the good;
Never against a mercy,
Against a right it stood;
And seeing this, that virtue
Is always friend to all,
The virtuous and true-hearted,
Men their protectors call.

# SELECTIONS FROM THE RAMAYANA

## EPIC OF RAMA, PRINCE OF INDIA

### I

### THE BRIDAL OF SITA

#### THE BREAKING OF THE BOW

JANAK, monarch of Videha, spake his message near and far, —
He shall win my peerless Sita, who shall bend my bow of war, —

Suitors came from farthest regions, warlike princes known to fame,
Vainly strove to wield the weapon, left Videha in their shame.

Viswa-mitra, royal *rishi*, Rama true and Lakshman bold,
Came to fair Mithila's city from Ayodhya famed of old.

Spake in pride the royal *rishi:* "Monarch of Videha's throne,
Grant, the wondrous bow of Rudra be to princely Rama shown."

Janak spake his royal mandate to his lords and
   warriors bold:
"Bring ye forth the bow of Rudra decked in garlands and in gold!"

And his peers and proud retainers waiting on the
   monarch's call,
Brought the great and goodly weapon from the
   city's inner hall.

Stalwart men of ample stature pulled the mighty
   iron car,
In which rested all-inviolate Janak's dreaded bow
   of war,

And where midst assembled monarchs sat Videha's
   godlike king,
With a mighty toil and effort did the eight-wheeled
   chariot bring.

"This the weapon of Videha," proudly thus the
   peers begun,
"Be it shewn to royal Rama, Dasa-ratha's righteous
   son!"

"This the bow," then spake the monarch to the
   *rishi* famed of old,
To the true and righteous Rama and to Lakshman young and bold,

"This the weapon of my fathers prized by kings
   from age to age;
Mighty chiefs and sturdy warriors could not bend
   it, noble sage!

Gods before the bow of RUDRA have in righteous terror quailed,
*Rakshas* fierce and stout *Asuras* have in futile effort failed,

Mortal man will struggle vainly Rudra's wondrous bow to bend,
Vainly strive to string the weapon and the shining dart to send.

Holy saint and royal *rishi*, here is Janak's ancient bow,
Shew it to Ayodhya's princes, speak to them my kingly vow!"

Viswa-mitra humbly listened to the words the monarch said,
To the brave and righteous Rama, Janak's mighty bow displayed.

Rama lifted high the cover of the pond'rous iron car,
Gazed with conscious pride and prowess on the mighty bow of war.

"Let me," humbly spake the hero, "on this bow my fingers place,
Let me lift and bend the weapon, help me with your loving grace."

"Be it so," the *rishi* answered, "Be it so," the monarch said.
Rama lifted high the weapon on his stalwart arms displayed,

Wond'ring gazed the kings assembled as the son of Raghu's race
Proudly raised the bow of Rudra with a warrior's stately grace,

Proudly strung the bow of Rudra which the kings had tried in vain,
Drew the cord with force resistless till the weapon snapped in twain!

Like the thunder's pealing accent rose the loud, terrific clang,
And the firm earth shook and trembled and the hills in echoes rang,

And the chiefs and gathered monarchs fell and fainted in their fear,
And the men of many nations shook, the dreadful sound to hear!

Pale and white the startled monarchs slowly from their terror woke,
And with royal grace and greetings Janak to the *rishi* spoke:

"Now my ancient eyes have witnessed wond'rous deed by Rama done,
Deed surpassing thought or fancy wrought by Dasa-ratha's son,

And the proud and peerless princess, Sita, glory of my house,
Sheds on me an added lustre as she weds a godlike spouse.

True shall be my plighted promise: Sita, dearer
than my life,
Won by worth and wond'rous valour shall be
Rama's faithful wife!

Grant us leave, O royal *rishi*, grant us blessings
kind and fair,
Envoys mounted on my chariot to Ayodhya shall
repair,

They shall speak to Rama's father glorious feat
by Rama done,
They shall speak to Dasa-ratha, Sita is by valour
won,

They shall say the noble princes safely live within
our walls,
They shall ask him by his presence to adorn our
palace halls!"

Pleased at heart the sage assented, envoys by the
monarch sent,
To Ayodhya's distant city with the royal message
went.

## The Wedding

SAGE Vasishtha skilled in duty placed Videha's
honoured king,
Viswa-mitra, Sata-manda, all within the sacred
ring,

And he raised the holy altar as the ancient writs
ordain,

Decked and graced with scented garlands grateful unto gods and men,
And he set the golden ladles, vases pierced by artists skilled,
Holy censers fresh and fragrant, cups with sacred honey filled,
*Sanka* bowls and shining salvers, *argbya* plates for honoured guest,
Parchéd rice arranged in dishes, corn unhusked that filled the rest,
And with careful hand Vasishtha grass around the altar flung,
Offered gift to lighted AGNI and the sacred *mantra* sung!
Softly came the sweet-eyed Sita, — bridal blush upon her brow, —
Rama in his manly beauty came to take the sacred vow,
Janak placed his beauteous daughter facing Dasaratha's son,
Spake with father's fond emotion and the holy rite was done;
"*This is Sita, child of Janak, dearer unto him than life,*
*Henceforth sharer of thy virtue, be she, prince, thy faithful wife,*
*Of thy weal and woe partaker, be she thine in every land,*

*Cherish her in joy and sorrow, clasp her hand within thy hand,*

*As the shadow to the substance, to her lord is faithful wife,*

*And my Sita best of women follows thee in death or life!"*

Tears bedew his ancient bosom, gods and men his wishes share,

And he sprinkles holy water on the blest and wedded pair.

Next he turned to Sita's sister, Urmila of beauty rare,

And to Lakshman young and valiant spake in accents soft and fair:

*"Lakshman, dauntless in thy duty, loved of men and Gods above,*

*Take my dear devoted daughter, Urmila of stainless love,*

*Lakshman, fearless in thy virtue, take thy true and faithful wife,*

*Clasp her hand within thy fingers, be she thine in death or life!"*

To his brother's child Mandavi, Janak turned with father's love,

Yielded her to righteous Bharat, prayed for blessings from above:

*"Bharat, take the fair Mandavi, be she thine in death or life,*

*Clasp her hand within thy fingers as thy true and faithful wife!"*

Last of all was Sruta-kriti, fair in form and fair in face,
And her gentle name was honoured for her acts of righteous grace,

*"Take her by the hand, Satrughna, be she thine in death or life,*
*As the shadow to the substance, to her lord is faithful wife!"*

Then the princes held the maidens, hand embraced in loving hand,
And Vasishtha spake the *mantra*, holiest priest in all the land.

Days of joy and months of gladness o'er the gentle Sita flew,
As she like the Queen of Beauty brighter in her graces grew,

And as VISHNU with his consort dwells in skies, alone, apart,
Rama in a sweet communion lived in Sita's loving heart!

## II
## THE BANISHMENT OF RAMA
### Dasa-ratha Chooses Rama as Regent

But of all his righteous children righteous
Rama won his heart,
As Swayambhu, of all creatures, was his dearest,
holiest part,

For his Rama strong and stately was his eldest
and his best,
Void of every baser passion and with every virtue
blest!

Soft in speech, sedate and peaceful, seeking still
the holy path,
Calm in conscious worth and valour, taunt nor
cavil waked his wrath,

In the field of war excelling, boldest warrior midst
the bold,
In the palace chambers musing on the tales by
elders told,

Faithful to the wise and learned, truthful in his
deed and word,
Rama dearly loved his people and his people
loved their lord!

To the Brahmans pure and holy Rama due obeisance made,
To the poor and to the helpless deeper love and
honour paid,

Spirit of his race and nation was to high-souled
  Rama given,
Thoughts that widen human glory, deeds that ope
  the gates of heaven!

Not intent on idle cavil Rama spake with purpose
  high,
And the God of speech might envy when he spake
  or made reply;
In the learning of the Vedas highest meed and
  glory won,
In the skill of arms the father scarcely matched
  the gallant son!

Taught by sages and by elders in the manners
  of his race,
Rama grew in social virtues and each soft endear-
  ing grace,
Taught by inborn pride and wisdom patient purpose to conceal,
Deep determined was his effort, dauntless was his
  silent will!

Dasa-ratha marked his Rama with each kingly
  virtue blest,
And from life-long royal duties now he sought
  repose and rest:
Shall I see my son anointed, seated on Kosala's
  throne,
In the evening of my life-time ere my days on
  earth be done,

Shall I place my ancient empire in the youthful Rama's care,
Seek for me a higher duty and prepare for life more fair?"

Pondering thus within his bosom counsel from his courtiers sought,
And to crown his Rama Regent was his purpose and his thought.

And he witnessed Rama's virtues filling all the world with love,
As the full-moon's radiant lustre fills the earth from skies above!

Dear to him appeared his purpose, Rama to his people dear,
Private wish and public duty made his path serene and clear.

### Intrigue

In the inner palace chamber stood the proud and peerless queen,
With a mother's joy Kaikeyi gaily watched the festive scene,

But with deep and deadly hatred Manthara, her nurse and maid,
Marked the city bright with banners, and in scornful accents said:

"Take thy presents back, Kaikeyi, for they ill befit the day,

And when clouds of sorrow darken, ill beseems
  thee to be gay,
And thy folly moves my laughter though an
  anguish wakes my sigh,
For a gladness stirs thy bosom when thy greatest
  woe is nigh!
Who that hath a woman's wisdom, who that is a
  prudent wife,
Smiles in joy when prouder rival triumphs in the
  race of life,
How can hapless Queen Kaikeyi greet this deed
  of darkness done,
When the favoured Queen Kausalya wins the empire for her son?
Happy is the Queen Kausalya in her regal pomp
  and state,
And Kaikeyi like a bond-slave must upon her
  rival wait!
Wilt thou do her due obeisance as we humble
  women do,
Will thy proud and princely Bharat as his brother's
  henchman go,
Will thy Bharat's gentle consort, fairest princess
  in this land,
In her tears and in her anguish wait on Sita's
  proud command?"
With a woman's scornful anger Manthara pro-
  claimed her grief,

With a mother's love for Rama thus Kaikeyi
answered brief:

"What inspires thee, wicked woman, thus to rail
in bitter tone,
Shall not Rama, best and eldest, fill his father's
royal throne,
What alarms thee, crooked woman, in the happy
rites begun,
Shall not Rama guard his brothers as a father
guards his son?" —

Scorn and anger shook her person and her bosom
heaved a sigh,
As in wilder, fiercer accents Manthara thus made
reply:

"But a danger thus ariseth if the elder wins the
throne;
Haste thee, heedless Queen Kaikeyi, save the
younger and thy son!
Speak thy mandate to thy husband, let thy
Bharat rule at home,
In the deep and pathless jungle let the banished
Rama roam,
This will please thy ancient father and thy father's
kith and kin,
This will please the righteous people, Bharat
knows no guile or sin!
Speak thy mandate to thy husband, win thy son
a happy fate,

Doom him not to Rama's service or his unrelent-
   ing hate,
Let not Rama in his rancour shed a younger
   brother's blood,
As the lion slays the tiger in the deep and echoing
   wood!
With the magic of thy beauty thou hast won thy
   monarch's heart,
Queen Kausalya's bosom rankles with a woman's
   secret smart,
Let her not with woman's vengeance turn upon
   her prouder foe,
And as crowned Rama's mother venge her in
   Kaikeyi's woe.
Mark my word, my child Kaikeyi, must these
   ancient eyes have seen,
Rama's rule is death to Bharat, insult to my
   honoured Queen!"
Like a slow but deadly poison worked the ancient
   nurse's tears,
And a wife's undying impulse mingled with a
   mother's fears,
Deep within Kaikeyi's bosom worked a woman's
   jealous thought,
Speechless in her scorn and anger mourner's
   dark retreat she sought.

## The King Seeks the Queen

THROUGH the portico of splendour graced by
  silver, tusk and gold,
Radiant with his thought of gladness walked the
  monarch proud and bold.
Through the lines of scented blossoms which by
  limpid waters shone,
And the rooms with seats of silver, ivory bench
  and golden throne,
Through the chamber of confection, where each
  viand wooed the taste,
Every object in profusion as in regions of the blest,
Through Kaikeyi's inner closet lighted with a
  softened sheen,
Walked the king with eager longing, — but Kaikeyi was not seen!
Thoughts of love and gentle dalliance woke within
  his ancient heart,
And the magic of her beauty and the glamour of
  her art.
With a soft desire the monarch vainly searched
  the vanished fair,
Found her not in royal chamber, found her not
  in gay parterre!
Filled with love and longing languor loitered not
  the radiant queen,
In her soft, voluptuous chamber, in the garden,
  grove or green,

And he asked the faithful warder of Kaikeyi, loved
    and lost,
She who served him with devotion and his wishes
    never crost.

Spake the warder in his terror that the queen,
    with rage distraught,
Weeping silent tears of anguish had the mourner's
    chamber sought.

Thither flew the stricken monarch; on the bare
    and unswept ground
Trembling with tumultuous passion was the Queen
    Kaikeyi found,

On the cold, uncovered pavement sorrowing lay
    the weeping wife,
Young wife of an ancient husband, dearer than his
    heart and life!

"Wherefore thus, my Queen and Empress, sorrow-
    laden in thy heart,
Who with daring slight or insult seeks to cause
    thy bosom smart?

Speak, command thy king's obedience, and thy
    wrath will melt away,
Like the melting snow of winter 'neath the sun's
    reviving ray!"

Blinded was the ancient husband as he lifted up
    her head,
Heedless oath and word he plighted that her wish
    should be obeyed.

### The Queen's Demand

Scheming for a fatal purpose, inly then Kaikeyi smiled,
And by sacred oath and promise bound the monarch love-beguiled:

"Thou hast given, Dasa-ratha, troth and word and royal oath,
Three and thirty Gods be witness, watchers of the righteous truth,

Sun and Moon and Stars be witness, Sky and Day and sable Night,
Rolling Worlds and this our wide Earth, and each dark and unseen wight,

Witness Rangers of the forest, Household Gods that guard us both,
Mortal beings and Immortal, — witness ye the monarch's oath,

Ever faithful to his promise, ever truthful in his word,
Dasa-ratha grants my prayer, Spirits and the Gods have heard!

Call to mind, O righteous monarch, days when in a bygone strife,
Warring with thy foes immortal thou hadst almost lost thy life,

With a woman's loving tendance poor Kaikeyi cured thy wound,

RAMA AND SITA ENTHRONED ATTENDED BY RAMA'S THREE BROTHERS AND THE FAITHFUL HANAUMAN RECEIVING HIS ORDERS

*From an Oriental Painting in the British Museum*

Till from death and danger rescued, thou wert
  by a promise bound,
Two rewards my husband offered, what my loving
  heart might seek,
Long delayed their wished fulfilment, — now let
  poor Kaikeyi speak,
And if royal deeds redeem not what thy royal
  lips did say,
Victim to thy broken promise Queen Kaikeyi
  dies to-day!

*By these rites ordained for Rama, — such the news
  my menials bring, —*
*Let my Bharat, and not Rama, be anointed Regent
  King,*
*Wearing skins and matted tresses, in the cave or
  hermit's cell,*
*Fourteen years in Dandak's forests let the elder
  Rama dwell,*
*These are Queen Kaikeyi's wishes, these are boons
  for which I pray,*
*I would see my son anointed, Rama banished on
  this day!"*

## The King's Lament

WHEREFORE now this cruel purpose hath a
  stainless heart defiled,
Ruthless wish to send my Rama to the dark and
  pathless wild?

Wherefore, darkly-scheming woman, on unrighteous purpose bent,
Doth thy cruel causeless vengeance on my Rama seek a vent,
Wherefore seek by deeds unholy for thy son the throne to win,
Throne which Bharat doth not covet, — blackened by his mother's sin?

Shall I see my banished Rama mantled in the garb of woe,
Reft of home and kin and empire to the pathless jungle go,
Shall I see disasters sweeping o'er my empire dark and deep,
As the forces of a foeman o'er a scattered army sweep?

Shall I hear assembled monarchs in their whispered voices say,
Weak and foolish in his dotage, Dasa-ratha holds his sway,
Shall I say to righteous elders when they blame my action done,
That by woman's mandate driven I have banished thus my son?

Queen Kausalya, dear-loved woman! she who serves me as a slave,
Soothes me like a tender sister, helps me like a consort brave,

As a fond and loving mother tends me with a watchful care,
As a daughter ever duteous doth obeisance sweet and fair,
When my fond and fair Kausalya asks me of her banished son,
How shall Dasa-ratha answer for the impious action done,—

How can husband, cold and cruel, break a wife's confiding heart,
How can father, false and faithless, from his best and eldest part?"

Coldly spake the Queen Kaikeyi: "If thy royal heart repent,
Break thy word and plighted promise, let thy royal faith be rent.

Truth-abiding is our monarch, so I heard the people say,
And his word is all inviolate, stainless virtue marks his sway.

Let it now be known to nations, — righteous Dasa-ratha lied,
And a trusting, cheated woman broke her loving heart and died!"

Darker grew the shades of midnight, coldly shone each distant star,
Wilder in the monarch's bosom raged the struggle and the war:

"Starry midnight, robed in shadows! give my wearied heart relief,
Spread thy sable covering mantle o'er an impious monarch's grief,

Spread thy vast and inky darkness o'er a deed of nameless crime,
Reign perennial o'er my sorrows heedless of the lapse of time,

May a sinful monarch perish ere the dawning of the day,
O'er a dark life sin-polluted, beam not morning's righteous ray!"

### The Sentence

MORNING came and duteous Rama to the palace bent his way,
For to make his salutation and his due obeisance pay,

And he saw his aged father shorn of kingly pomp and pride,
And he saw the Queen Kaikeyi sitting by her consort's side.

Duteously the righteous Rama touched the ancient monarch's feet,
Touched the feet of Queen Kaikeyi with a son's obeisance meet.

"Rama!" cried the feeble monarch, but the tear bedimmed his eye,

Sorrow choked his failing utterance and his bosom heaved a sigh.

Rama started in his terror at his father's grief or wrath,
Like a traveller in the jungle crossed by serpent in his path,
Reft of sense appeared the monarch, crushed beneath a load of pain,
Heaving oft a sigh of sorrow as his heart would break in twain,
Like the ocean tempest-shaken, like the sun in eclipse pale,
Like a crushed, repenting "rishi" when his truth and virtue fail!

Breathless mused the anxious Rama, — what foul action hath he done,
What strange anger fills his father, wherefore greets he not his son?

"Speak, my mother," uttered Rama, "what strange error on my part,
Unremembered sin or folly fills with grief my father's heart?

Gracious unto me is father with a father's boundless grace,
Wherefore clouds his altered visage, wherefore tears bedew his face?

Speak, my ever-loving mother, speak the truth for thou must know,

What distress or deep disaster pains his heart and clouds his brow?"

Mother's love nor woman's pity moved the deep-determined queen,
As in cold and cruel accents thus she spake her purpose keen:

"Grief nor woe nor sudden ailment pains thy father loved of old,
But he fears to speak his purpose to his Rama true and bold,
And his loving accents falter some unloving wish to tell,
Till you give your princely promise, you will serve his mandate well!

Listen more, in bygone seasons, — Rama, thou wert then unborn, —
I had saved thy royal father, he a gracious boon had sworn,
But his feeble heart repenting, is by pride and passion stirred,
He would break his royal promise as a caitiff breaks his word.

Years have passed and now the monarch would his ancient word forego,
He would build a needless causeway when the waters ceased to flow!

Truth inspires each deed attempted and each word by monarchs spoke,

Not for thee, though loved and honoured, should a royal vow be broke,

If the true and righteous Rama binds him by his father's vow,
I will tell thee of the anguish which obscures his royal brow;

If thy feeble bosom falter and thy halting purpose fail,
Unredeemed is royal promise and unspoken is my tale!"

"Speak thy word," exclaimed the hero, "and my purpose shall not fail,
Rama serves his father's mandate and his bosom shall not quail,

Poisoned cup or death untimely, — what the cruel fates decree, —
To his king and to his father Rama yields obedience free,

Speak my father's royal promise, hold me by his promise tied,
Rama speaks and shall not palter, for his lips have never lied."

Cold and clear Kaikeyi's accents fell as falls the hunter's knife,
"Listen then to word of promise and redeem it with thy life.

Wounded erst by foes immortal, saved by Queen Kaikeyi's care,

Two great boons your father plighted and his
  royal words were fair.
I have sought their due fulfilment, — brightly
  shines my Bharat's star, —
Bharat shall be Heir and Regent, Rama shall be
  banished far!

*If thy father's royal mandate thou wouldst list and
  honor still,*
*Fourteen years in Dandak's forest live and wander
  at thy will,*

*Seven long years and seven, my Rama, thou shalt in
  the jungle dwell,*
*Bark of trees shall be thy raiment and thy home the
  hermit's cell.*

*Over fair Kosala's empire let my princely Bharat
  reign,*
*With his cars and steeds and tuskers, wealth and gold
  and arméd men!*

Tender-hearted is the monarch, age and sorrow
  dim his eye,
And the anguish of a father checks his speech and
  purpose high,

For the love he bears thee, Rama, cruel vow he
  may not speak,
I have spoke his will and mandate, and thy true
  obedience seek."

Calmly Rama heard the mandate, grief nor anger touched his heart,
Calmly from his father's empire and his home prepared to part.

### III

### THE PARTING

#### Rama takes Leave from Sita

Dearly loved, devoted Sita! daughter of a royal line,
Part we now, for years of wand'ring in the pathless woods is mine,
For my father, promise-fettered, to Kaikeyi yields the sway,
And she wills her son anointed, — fourteen years doth Rama stray,
But before I leave thee, Sita, in the wilderness to rove,
Yield me one more tender token of thy true and trustful love!
Serve my crownéd brother, Sita, as a faithful, duteous dame,
Tell him not of Rama's virtues, tell him not of Rama's claim,
Since my royal father willeth, — Bharat shall be regent-heir,
Serve him with a loyal duty, serve him with obeisance fair;

Since my royal father willeth, — years of banishment be mine,
Brave in sorrow and in suffering, woman's brightest fame be thine!

Keep thy fasts and vigils, Sita, while thy Rama is away,
Faith in Gods and faith in virtue on thy bosom hold their sway,

In the early watch of morning to the Gods for blessings pray,
To my father, Dasa-ratha, honour and obeisance pay,

To my mother, Queen Kausalya, is thy dearest tendance due,
Offer her thy consolation, be a daughter fond and true!

Listen, Sita, unto Bharat speak no heedless angry word,
He is monarch of Kosala and of Raghu's race is lord,

Crownéd kings our willing service and our faithful duty own,
Dearest sons they disinherit, cherish strangers near the throne!

Bharat's will with deep devotion and with faultless faith obey,
Truth and virtue on thy bosom ever hold their gentle sway,

And to please each dear relation, gentle Sita, be it thine;
Part we, love! for years of wand'ring in the pathless woods is mine!"

## Woman's Love

RAMA spake, and soft-eyed Sita, ever sweet in speech and word,
Stirred by loving woman's passion boldly answered thus her lord:

"Do I hear my husband rightly, are these words my Rama spake,
And her banished lord and husband will the wedded wife forsake?

Lightly I dismiss the counsel which my lord hath lightly said,
For it ill beseems a warrior and my husband's princely grade!

*For the faithful woman follows where her wedded lord may lead,*
*In the banishment of Rama, Sita's exile is decreed.*

*Sire nor son nor loving brother rules the wedded woman's state,*
*With her lord she falls or rises, with her consort courts her fate.*

*If the righteous son of Raghu wends to forests dark and drear,*

*Sita steps before her husband wild and thorny paths to clear!*

Car and steed and gilded palace, vain are these to woman's life,
Dearer is her husband's shadow to the loved and loving wife!

For my mother often taught me and my father often spake,
That her home the wedded woman doth beside her husband make,

As the shadow to the substance, to her lord is faithful wife,
And she parts not from her consort till she parts with fleeting life!

Therefore bid me seek the jungle and in pathless forests roam,
Where the wild deer freely ranges and the tiger makes his home.

Happier than in father's mansions in the woods will Sita rove,
Waste no thought on home or kindred, nestling in her husband's love!

Bid me seek the sylvan greenwoods, wooded hills and plateaus high,
Limpid rills and crystal *nullas* as they softly ripple by,
And where in the lake of lotus tuneful ducks their plumage lave.

Let me with my loving Rama skim the cool translucent wave!

Years will pass in happy union, — happiest lot to woman given, —
Sita seeks not throne or empire, nor the brighter joys of heaven.

Heaven conceals not brighter mansions in its sunny fields of pride,
Where without her lord and husband faithful Sita would reside!"

### Brother's Faithfulness

TEARS bedewed the face of Lakshman as he heard what Sita said,
And he touched the feet of Rama and in gentle accents prayed:

*"If my elder and his lady to the pathless forests wend,*
*Armed with bow and ample quiver Lakshman will on them attend,*

*Where the wild deer range the forest and the lordly tuskers roam,*
*And the bird of gorgeous plumage nestles in its jungle home.*

*Dearer far to me these woodlands where my elder Rama dwells,*
*Than the homes of bright Immortals where perennial bliss prevails!*

Grant me then thy sweet permission, — faithful to thy glorious star,
Lakshman shall not wait and tarry when his Rama wanders far,

Grant me then thy loving mandate, — Lakshman hath no wish to stay,
None shall bar the faithful younger when the elder leads the way!"

## IV

### IN THE FOREST. SITA LOST

#### Surpa-nakha in Love

As the Moon with starry Chitra dwells in azure skies above,
In his lonesome leafy cottage Rama dwelt in Sita's love,

And with Lakshman strong and valiant, quick to labour and obey,
Tales of bygone times recounting Rama passed the livelong day.

And it so befell, a maiden, dweller of the darksome wood,
Led by wand'ring thought or fancy once before the cottage stood,

Surpa-nakha, Raksha maiden, sister of the Raksha lord,
Came and looked with eager longing till her soul was passion-stirred!

Looked on Rama lion-chested, mighty-armèd, lotus-eyed,
Stately as the jungle tusker, with his crown of tresses tied,

Looked on Rama lofty-fronted, with a royal visage graced,
Like Kandarpa young and lustrous, lotus-hued and lotus-faced!

What though she a Raksha maiden, poor in beauty, plain in face,
Fell her glances passion-laden on the prince of peerless grace,

What though wild her eyes and tresses, and her accents counselled fear,
Soft-eyed Rama fired her bosom, and his sweet voice thrilled her ear,

What though bent on deeds unholy, holy Rama won her heart,
And, for love makes bold a female, thus did she her thoughts impart:

"Who be thou in hermit's vestments, in thy native beauty bright,
Friended by a youthful woman, armèd with thy bow of might,

Who be thou in these lone regions where the Rakshas hold their sway,
Wherefore in a lonely cottage in this darksome jungle stay?"

With his wonted truth and candour Rama spake
sedate and bold,
And the story of his exile to the Raksha maiden
told:

"Dasa-ratha of Ayodhya ruled with Indra's godlike fame,
And his eldest, first born, Rama, by his mandate
here I came,

Younger Lakshman strong and valiant doth with
me these forests roam,
And my wife, Videha's daughter, Sita makes with
me her home.

Duteous to my father's bidding, duteous to my
mother's will,
Striving in the cause of virtue in the woods we
wander still.

Tell me, female of the forest, who thou be and
whence thy birth,
Much I fear thou art a Raksha wearing various
forms on earth!"

"Listen," so spake Surpa-nakha, "if my purpose
thou wouldst know,
I am Raksha, Surpa-nakha, wearing various
shapes below,

Know my brothers, royal Ravan, Lanka's lord
from days of old,
Kumbha-karna dread and dauntless and Bibhishan true and bold,

Khara and the doughty Dushan with me in these
  forests stray,
But by Rama's love emboldened I have left them
  on the way!

Broad and boundless is my empire and I wander
  in my pride,
Thee I choose as lord and husband, — cast thy
  human wife aside.

Pale is Sita and misshapen, scarce a warrior's
  worthy wife,
To a nobler, lordlier female consecrate thy gallant life!

Human flesh is food of Rakshas! weakling Sita I
  will slay,
Slay that boy thy stripling brother, — thee as
  husband I obey,

On the peaks of lofty mountains, in the forests
  dark and lone,
We shall range the boundless woodlands and the
  joys of dalliance prove!"

Rama heard her impious purpose and a gentle
  smile repressed,
To the foul and forward female thus his mocking
  words addressed:

"List, O passion-smitten maiden! Sita is my
  honoured wife,
With a rival loved and cherished cruel were thy
  wedded life!

But no consort follows Lakshman, peerless is his
    comely face,
Dauntless is his warlike valour, matchless is his
    courtly grace,

And he leads no wife or consort to this darksome
    woodland grove,
With no rival to thy passion seek his ample-
    hearted love!"

Surpa-nakha passion-laden then on Lakshman
    turned her eye,
But in merry mocking accents smiling Lakshman
    made reply:

"Ruddy in thy youthful beauty like the lotus in
    her pride,
I am slave of royal Rama, would'st thou be a
    vassal's bride?

Rather be his younger consort, banish Sita from
    his arms,
Spurning Sita's faded beauty let him seek thy
    fresher charms,

Spurning Sita's faded graces let him brighter
    pleasures prove,
Wearied with a woman's dalliance let him court a
    Raksha's love!"

Wrath of unrequited passion raged like madness
    in her breast,
Torn by anger strong as tempest thus her answer
    she addrest:

"Are these mocking accents uttered, Rama, to insult my flame,
Feasting on her faded beauty dost thou still revere thy dame?
But beware a Raksha's fury and an injured female's wrath,
Surpa-nakha slays thy consort, bears no rival in her path!"

### Surpa-nakha's Revenge

THEN the humbled Surpa-nakha to her royal brother hied,
Spake her sorrows unto Ravan and Maricha true and tried.
Shape of deer unmatched in beauty now the deep Maricha wore,
Golden tints upon his haunches, sapphire on his antlers bore,
Till the woodland-wand'ring Sita marked the creature in his pride,
Golden was his neck of beauty, silver white his flank and side!

"Come, my lord and gallant Lakshman," thus the raptur'd Sita spake,
"Mark the deer of wondrous radiance browsing by the forest brake!"

"Much my heart misgives me, sister," Lakshman hesitated still,

"'Tis some deep deceitful Raksha wearing every shape at will,

Monarchs wand'ring in this forest, hunting in this lonely glen,

Oft waylaid by artful Rakshas are by deep devices slain,

Bright as day-god or *Gandharva*, woodland scenes they love to stray,

Till they fall upon the heedless, quick to slaughter and to slay.

Trust me, not in jewelled lustre forest creatures haunt the green,

'Tis some *maya* and illusion, trust not what thy eyes have seen!"

Vainly spake the watchful Lakshman in the arts of Rakshas skilled,

For with forceful fascination Sita's inmost heart was thrilled.

"Husband, good and ever gracious," sweetly thus implored the wife,

"I would tend this thing of beauty, — sharer of my forest life!

I have witnessed in this jungle graceful creatures passing fair,

*Chowri* and the gentle roebuck, antelope of beauty rare,

I have seen the lithesome monkey sporting in the branches' shade,

Grizzly bear that feeds on *Mahua*, and the deer that crops the blade,
I have marked the stately wild bull dash into the deepest wood,
And the *Kinnar* strange and wondrous as in sylvan wilds he stood,
But these eyes have never rested on a form so wondrous fair,
On a shape so full of beauty, decked with tints so rich and rare!
If alive this wary creature be it, husband, hard to take,
Slay him and his skin of lustre cherish for thy Sita's sake.
I will as a golden carpet spread the skin upon the grass,
Sweet memento of this forest when our forest days will pass!"
Rama bade the faithful Lakshman with the gentle Sita stay,
Long through woods and gloomy gorges vainly held his cautious way,
Vainly set the snare in silence by the lake and in the dale,
'Scaping every trap, Maricha, pierced by Rama's arrows fell,
Imitating Rama's accents uttered forth his dying cry:

"Speed, my faithful brother Lakshman, helpless in the woods I die!"

## Lakshman's Departure

Heardst that distant cry of danger?" questioned Sita in distress,
"Woe, to me! who in my frenzy sent my lord to wilderness,

Speed, brave Lakshman, help my Rama, doleful was his distant cry,
And my fainting bosom falters and a dimness clouds my eye!

To the dread and darksome forest with thy keenest arrows speed,
Help thy elder and thy monarch, sore his danger and his need,

For perchance the cruel Rakshas gather round his lonesome path,
As the mighty bull is slaughtered by the lions in their wrath!"

Spake the hero: "Fear not, Sita! Dwellers of the azure height,
Rakshas nor the jungle-rangers match the peerless Rama's might,

Rama knows no dread or danger, and his mandate still I own,
And I may not leave thee, Lady, in this cottage all alone!

Cast aside thy causeless terror; in the sky or earth below,
In the nether regions, Rama knows no peer or equal foe,
He shall slay the deer of jungle, he shall voice no dastard cry,
'Tis some trick of wily Rakshas in this forest dark and high!

Sita, thou hast heard my elder bid me in this cottage stay,
Lakshman may not leave thee, Lady, for his duty — to obey,
Ruthless Rakshas roam the forest to revenge their leader slain,
Various are their arts and accents; chase thy thought of causeless pain!"

Sparkled Sita's eye in anger, frenzy marked her speech and word,
For a woman's sense is clouded by the danger of her lord:

"Markest thou my Rama's danger with a cold and callous heart,
Courtest thou the death of elder in thy deep deceitful art,
In thy semblance of compassion dost thou hide a cruel craft,
As in friendly guise the foeman hides his death-compelling shaft,

Following like a faithful younger in this dread and
    lonesome land,
Seekest thou the death of elder to enforce his
    widow's hand?

False thy hope as foul thy purpose! Sita is a
    faithful wife,
Sita follows saintly Rama, true in death as true
    in life!"

"Daughter of Videha's monarch, — pardon if I
    do thee wrong, —
Fickle is the faith of woman, poison-dealing is
    her tongue!

And thy censure, trust me, Lady, scathes me like
    a burning dart,
Free from guile is Lakshman's purpose, free from
    sin is Lakshman's heart.

Witness ye my truth of purpose, unseen dwellers
    of the wood,
Witness, I for Sita's safety by my elder's mandate
    stood,

Duteous to my queen and elder, I have toiled and
    worked in vain,
Dark suspicion and dishonour cast on me a need-
    less stain!

*Lady! I obey thy mandate, to my elder now I
    go,*
*Guardian Spirits of the forest watch thee from each
    secret foe,*

*Omens dark and signs of danger meet my pained and aching sight,*
*May I see thee by thy Rama, guarded by his conquering might!"*

### Ravan's Coming

RAVAN watched the happy moment burning with a vengeful spite,
Came to sad and sorrowing Sita in the guise of anchorite,
Tufted hair and russet garment, sandals on his feet he wore,
And depending from his shoulders on a staff his vessel bore.

And he came to lonely Sita, for each warlike chief was gone,
As the darkness comes to evening lightless from the parted Sun.

Mute and still were forest creatures when in guise of anchorite,
Unto Sita's lonely cottage pressed the Raksha in his might,
Mute and voiceless was the jungle as he cast on her his eye,
As across the star of Chitra planet Sani walks the sky!

Ravan stood in hermit's vestments, — vengeful purpose unrevealed, —

As a deep and darksome cavern is by grass and
leaf concealed,
Ravan stood sedate and silent, and he gazed on
Rama's queen,
Ivory brow and lip of coral, sparkling teeth of
pearly sheen!
Lighting up the lonely cottage Sita sat in radiance
high,
As the Moon with streaks of silver fills the lonely
midnight sky,
Lighting up the gloomy woodlands with her eyes
serenely fair,
With her bark-clad shape of beauty mantled by
her raven hair!
Ravan fired by impure passion fixed on her his
lustful eye,
And the light that lit his glances gave his holy
texts the lie,
Ravan in his flattering accents, with a soft and
soothing art,
Praised the woman's peerless beauty to subdue
the woman's heart.

"Art thou *Sri* or radiant *Gauri*, maid of Fortune
or of Fame,
Nymph of Love or sweet Fruition, what may be
thy sacred name?
On thy lips of ruddy coral teeth of tender jasmine
shine,

In thy eyes of limpid lustre dwells a light of love
  divine,

Tall and slender, softly rounded, are thy limbs of
  beauty rare,
Like the swelling fruit of *tala* heaves thy bosom
  sweetly fair!

Goddess or Gandharva maiden wears no brighter
  form or face,
Woman seen by eyes of mortals owns not such
  transcendent grace,

Wherefore, then, in lonesome forest, nymph or
  maiden, make thy stay,
Where the jungle creatures wander and the Rakshas hold their sway?

Royal halls and stately mansions were for thee a
  meeter home,
And thy steps should grace a palace, not in pathless forest roam,

Blossoms rich, not thorn of jungle, decorate a
  lady's bower,
Silken robes, not sylvan garments, heighten
  beauty's potent power!

Lady of the sylvan forest! other destiny is thine, —
As a bride beloved and courted in thy bridal garments shine,

Choose a loved and lordly suitor who shall wait
  on thee in pride,

Choose a hero worth thy beauty, be a monarch's
  queenly bride!

Speak thy lineage, heaven-descended! who may
  be thy parents high,
*Rudras* or the radiant *Maruts*, *Vasus* leaders of
  the sky,

All unworthy is this forest for a nymph or heavenly
  maid,
Beasts of prey infest the jungle, Rakshas haunt
  its gloomy shade,

Lions dwell in lonely caverns, tuskers ford the
  silent lake,
Monkeys sport on pendant branches, tigers steal
  beneath the brake,

Wherefore then this dismal forest doth thy fairy
  face adorn,
Who art thou and whence descended, nymph or
  maid or goddess-born?"

## Ravan's Wooing

LISTEN, Brahman!" answered Sita, — unsus-
  pecting in her mind
That she saw a base betrayer in a hermit seeming
  kind, —

"I am born of royal Janak, ruler of Videha's land,
Rama prince of proud Kosala by his valour won
  my hand.

Years we passed in peaceful pleasure in Ayodya's
  happy clime,
Rich in every rare enjoyment gladsome passed
  our happy time,
Till the monarch Dasa-ratha, — for his days were
  almost done, —
Wished to crown the royal Rama as his Heir and
  Regent son.

But the scheming Queen Kaikeyi claimed a long-
  forgotten boon,
That my consort should be exiled and her son
  should fill the throne,
She would take no rest or slumber, nourishment
  of drink or food,
Till her Bharat ruled the empire, Rama banished
  to the wood!

Lion in his warlike valour, hermit in his saintly
  vow,
Lakshman with his honoured elder wanders
  through the forest now.

Rest thee here, O holy Brahman, rich in piety and
  fame,
Till the forest-ranging brothers greet thee with
  the forest game,
Speak, if so it please thee, father, what great *rishi*
  claims thy birth,
Wherefore in this pathless jungle wand'rest friend-
  less on this earth?"

"Brahman nor a righteous *rishi*," royal Ravan made reply,
"Leader of the wrathful Rakshas, Lanka's lord and king am I,
He whose valour quells the wide-world, Gods above and men below,
He whose proud and peerless prowess Rakshas and Asuras know!

But thy beauty's golden lustre, Sita, wins my royal heart,
Be a sharer of my empire, of my glory take a part,

Many queens of queenly beauty on the royal Ravan wait,
Thou shalt be their reigning empress, thou shalt own my regal state!

Lanka girt by boundless ocean is of royal towns the best,
Seated in her pride and glory on a mountain's towering crest,

And in mountain paths and woodlands thou shalt with thy Ravan stray,
Not in Godavari's gorges through the dark and dreary day,

And five thousand gay-dressed damsels shall upon my Sita wait,
Queen of Ravan's true affection, proud partaker of his state!"

Sparkled Sita's eyes in anger and a tremor shook
  her frame,
As in proud and scornful accents answered thus
  the royal dame:

"Know'st thou Rama great and godlike, peerless
  hero in the strife,
Deep, uncompassed, like the ocean? — I am
  Rama's wedded wife!

Know'st thou Rama proud and princely, sinless
  in his saintly life,
Stately as the tall *Nyagradha?* — I am Rama's
  wedded wife!

Mighty-arméd, mighty-chested, mighty with his
  bow and sword,
Lion midst the sons of mortals, — Rama is my
  wedded lord!

Stainless as the Moon in glory, stainless in his
  deed and word,
Rich in valour and in virtue, — Rama is my
  wedded lord!

Sure thy fitful life is shadowed by a dark and
  dreadful fate,
Since in frenzy of thy passion courtest thou a
  warrior's mate,

Tear the tooth of hungry lion while upon the calf
  he feeds,
Touch the fang of deadly cobra while his dying
  victim bleeds,

Aye uproot the solid mountain from its base of rocky land,
Ere thou win the wife of Rama, stout of heart and strong of hand!

Hurl thyself upon the ocean from a towering peak and high,
Snatch the orbs of day and midnight from their spheres in azure sky,

Tongues of flaming conflagration in thy flowing dress enfold,
Ere thou take the wife of Rama to thy distant dungeon hold,

Ere thou seek to insult Rama unrelenting in his wrath,
O'er a bed of pikes of iron tread a softer easier path!"

## Ravan's Triumph

VAIN her threat and soft entreaty, Ravan held her in his wrath,
As the planet Budha captures fair Rokini in his path,

By his left hand tremor-shaken, Ravan held her streaming hair,
By his right the ruthless Raksha lifted up the fainting fair!

Unseen dwellers of the woodlands watched the dismal deed of shame,

Marked the mighty-armed Raksha lift the poor and helpless dame,
Seat her on his car celestial yoked with *asses* winged with speed,
Golden in its shape and radiance, fleet as Indra's heavenly steed!

Angry threat and sweet entreaty Ravan to her ears addressed,
As the struggling fainting woman still he held upon his breast,
Vain his threat and vain entreaty, "Rama! Rama!" still she cried,
To the dark and distant forest where her noble lord had hied.

Then arose the car celestial o'er the hill and wooded vale,
Like a snake in eagle's talons Sita writhed with piteous wail,
Dim and dizzy, faint and faltering, still she sent her piercing cry,
Echoing through the boundless woodlands, pealing to the upper sky:

"Save me, mighty-arméd Lakshman, stainless in thy heart and deed,
Save a faithful wife and woman from a Raksha's lust and greed,

True and faithful was thy warning, — false and foul the charge I made,

Pardon, friend, an erring sister, pardon words a woman said!

Help me, ever righteous Rama, duty bade thee yield thy throne,
Duty bids thee smite the sinful, save the wife who is thy own,
Thou art king and stern chastiser of each deed of sin and shame,
Hurl thy vengeance on the Raksha who insults thy faithful dame!

*Deed of sin, unrighteous Ravan, brings in time its dreadful meed,*
*As the young corn grows and ripens from the small and living seed,*
*For this deed of insult, Ravan, in thy heedless folly done,*
*Death of all thy race and kindred thou shalt reap from Raghu's son!*

Ah, my Rama, mighty-armèd! vengeance soon shall speed thy way,
When thou hearest, helpless Sita is by Ravan torn away!

And thou royal bird, Jatayu, witness Ravan's deed of shame,
Witness how he courts destruction, stealing Rama's faithful dame,

Rama and the gallant Lakshman soon shall find their destined prey,

When they know that trusting Sita is by Ravan
 torn away!"
Vainly wept the anguished Sita; vain Jatayu in
 his wrath,
Fought with beak and bloody talons to impede
 the Raksha's path,
Pierced and bleeding fell the vulture; Ravan fled
 with Rama's bride,
Where amidst the boundless ocean Lanka rose in
 towering pride!

V

THE QUEST FOR SITA

FRIENDS IN MISFORTUNE

LONG and loud lamented Rama by his lonesome cottage door,
Janasthana's woodlands answered, Panchavati's
 echoing shore,
Long he searched in wood and jungle, mountain
 crest and pathless plain,
Till he reached the Malya mountains stretching
 to the southern main.

There Sugriva king of Vanars, Hanuman his
 henchman brave,
Banished from their home and empire lived within
 the forest cave,
To the exiled king Sugriva, Hanuman his purpose
 told,

As he marked the pensive Rama wand'ring with his brother bold:

"Mark the sons of Dasa-ratha banished from their royal home,
Duteous to their father's mandate in these pathless forests roam,

By a monarch's stainless duty people's love the monarch won,
By a woman's false contrivance banished he his eldest son!

True to duty, true to virtue, Rama passed his forest life,
Till a false perfidious Raksha stole his fair and faithful wife,

And the anguish-stricken husband seeks thy friendship and thy aid, —
Mutual sorrow blends your fortunes, be ye friends in mutual need!"

Bold Sugriva heard the counsel, and to righteous Rama hied,
And the princes of Ayodhya with his greetings gratified:

"*Well I know thee, righteous Rama, soul of piety and love,*
*And thy duty to thy father and thy faith in Gods above,*

*Fortune favours poor Sugriva, Rama courts his humble aid,*

*In our deepest direst danger be our truest friendships made!*

*Equal is our fateful fortune, — I have lost a queenly wife,*
*Banished from Kishkindha's empire here I lead a forest life,*
*Pledge of love and true alliance, Rama, take this proffered band,*
*Banded by a common sorrow we shall fall or stoutly stand!*

For my tyrant brother Bali rules Kishkindha all alone,
Forced my wife from my embraces, drove me from my father's throne,
Trembling in my fear and anguish I endure a life of woe,
Render me my wife and empire from my brother and my foe!"

"Not in vain they seek my succour," so the gallant Rama said,
"Who with love and offered friendship seek my counsel and my aid,
Not in vain these glistening arrows in my ample quiver shine,
Bali dies the death of tyrants, wife and empire shall be thine.

*Quick as* INDRA'S *forkéd lightning are these arrows feather-plumed,*

*Deadly as the hissing serpent are these darts with
   points illumed,*

*And this day shall not be ended ere it sees thy brother
   fall,*

*As by lurid lightning severed sinks the crest of mountain tall!* —

Ah, my lost and loving Sita! writhing in a Raksha's
   power,
As the lightning shakes and quivers in this dark
   tempestuous shower,
Shadows thicken on the prospect, flower and leaf
   are wet with rain,
And each passing object, Lakshman, wakes in me
   a thought of pain!
Joyously from throne and empire with my Sita I
   could part,
As the stream erodes its margin, Sita's absence
   breaks my heart!
Rain and tempest cloud the prospect as they
   cloud my onward path,
Dubious is my darksome future, mighty is my
   foeman's wrath!
Ravan monarch of the Rakshas, — so Jatayu said
   and died, —
In some unknown forest fastness doth my sorrowing Sita hide,
But Sugriva true and faithful seeks the Raksha's
   secret hold,

Firm in faith and fixed in purpose we will face our
   foeman bold!" —

Past the rains, the marshalled Vanars gathered
   round Sugriva bold,
And unto a gallant chieftain thus the king his
   purpose told:

"Brave in war and wise in counsel! take ten thousand of my best,
Seek the hiding-place of Ravan in the regions of
   the East.

Seek each ravine rock and forest and each shadowy
   hill and cave,
Far where bright Sarayu's waters mix with Ganga's
   ruddy wave,

And where Jumna's dark blue waters ceaseless roll
   in regal pride,
And the Sone through leagues of country spreads
   its torrent far and wide!" —

### SITA IN THE ASOKA GARDENS

CROSSED the ocean's boundless waters,
   Hanuman in duty brave,
Lighted on the emerald island girdled by the
   sapphire wave,

And in tireless quest of Sita searched the margin
   of the sea,
In a dark *Asoka* garden hid himself within a
   tree.

By the rich and royal mansion Hanuman his eyes did rest
On a woman sad and sorrowing in her sylvan garments drest,
Like the moon obscured and clouded, dim with shadows deep and dark,
Like the smoke-enshrouded red fire, dying with a feeble spark,
Like the tempest-pelted lotus by the wind and torrent shaken,
Like the beauteous star Rohini by a *graba* overtaken!

Fasts and vigils paled her beauty, tears bedimmed her tender grace,
Anguish dwelt within her bosom, sorrow darkened on her face,

And she lived by Rakshas guarded, as a faint and timid deer,
Severed from her herd and kindred when the prowling wolves are near,

And her raven locks ungathered hung behind in single braid,
And her gentle eye was lightless, and her brow was hid in shade!

"This is she! the peerless princess, Rama's consort loved and lost,
This is she! the saintly Sita, by a cruel fortune crost,"

Hanuman thus thought and pondered: "On her graceful form I spy,
Gems and gold by sorrowing Rama oft depicted with a sigh,
On her ears the golden pendants and the tiger's sharpened tooth,
On her arms the jewelled bracelets, tokens of unchanging truth,

On her pallid brow and bosom still the radiant jewels shine,
Rama with a sweet affection did in early days entwine!

Hermit's garments clothe her person, braided is her raven hair,
Matted bark of trees of forest drape her neck and bosom fair,

And a dower of dazzling beauty still bedecks her peerless face,
Though the shadowing tinge of sorrow darkens all her earlier grace!

This is she! the soft-eyed Sita, wept with unavailing tear,
This is she! the faithful consort, unto Rama ever dear,

Unforgetting and unchanging, truthful still in deed and word,
Sita in her silent suffering sorrows for her absent lord,

Still for Rama, lost but cherished, Sita heaves the choking sigh,
Sita lives for righteous Rama, for her Rama she would die!"

### Rama's Token

"'TIS no dream's deceitful whisper!" Hanuman spake to the dame,
As from darksome leafy shelter he to Rama's consort came,

"Rama's messenger and vassal, token from thy lord I bring,
Mark this bright ring, jewel-lettered with the dear name of thy king,

For the loved and cherished Sita is to Rama ever dear,
And he sends his loving message and his force is drawing near!"

Sita held that tender token from her loved and cherished lord,
And once more herself she fancied to his loving arms restored,

And her pallid face was lighted and her soft eye sent a spark,
As the Moon regains her lustre freed from *Rahu's* shadows dark!

And with voice of deep-emotion in each softly whispered word,

Spake her thoughts in gentle accents of her consort and her lord:

"Messenger of love of Rama! Dauntless is thy deed and bold,
Thou hast crossed the boundless ocean to the Raksha's castled hold,
Thou hast crossed the angry billows which confess no monarch's sway,
O'er the face of rolling waters found thy unresisted way,
Thou hast done what living mortal never sought to do before,
Dared the Raksha in his island, Ravan in his sea-girt shore!

Speak, if Rama lives in safety in the woods or by the hill,
And if young and gallant Lakshman faithful serves his brother still,
Speak, if Rama in his anger and his unforgiving ire,
Hurls destruction on my captor like the world-consuming fire?

Doth my husband seek alliance with each wild and warlike chief,
Striving for a speedy vengeance and for Sita's quick relief,
Doth he stir the warlike races to a fierce and vengeful strife,

Dealing death to ruthless Rakshas for this insult on his wife,

Doth he still in fond remembrance cherish Sita loved of yore,
Nursing in his hero-bosom tender sorrows evermore?" —

"I will swear, my gentle Lady, Rama's vengeance draweth nigh,
Thou shalt see his beaming visage like the Lord of Midnight Sky,

Firm in purpose Rama waiteth on the Prasravana hill,
As upon the huge Airavat, INDRA; motionless and still!

*Flesh of deer nor forest honey tasteth Rama true and bold,*
*Till he rescues cherished Sita from the Raksha's castled hold,*

*Thoughts of Sita leave not Rama dreary day or darksome night,*
*Till his vengeance deep and dreadful crushes Ravan in his might,*

*Forest flower nor scented creeper pleases Rama's anguished heart,*
*Till he wins his wedded consort by his death-compelling dart!"*

## Sita's Token

Token from her raven tresses Sita to the Vanar gave,
Hanuman with dauntless valour crossed once more the ocean wave,

Where in Prasra-vana's mountain Rama with his brother stayed,
Jewel from the brow of Sita by her sorrowing consort laid,

Spake of Ravan's foul endearment and his loathsome loving word,
Spake of Sita's scorn and anger and her truth unto her lord,

Tears of sorrow and affection from the warrior's eyelids start,
As his consort's loving token Rama presses to his heart!

"Hanuman, my friend and comrade, lead me to the distant isle,
Where my soft-eyed Sita lingers midst the Rakshas dark and vile,

Where my true and tender consort like a lone and stricken deer,
Girt by Rakshas stern and ruthless sheds the unavailing tear,

Where she weeps in ceaseless anguish, sorrow-stricken, sad and pale,
Like the Moon by dark clouds shrouded then her light and lustre fail!

Speak again, my faithful henchman, loving message of my wife,
Like some potent drug her accents renovate my fainting life,

Arm thy forces, friend Sugriva, Rama shall not brook delay,
While in distant Lanka's confines Sita weeps the livelong day,

Marshal forth thy bannered forces, cross the ocean in thy might,
Rama speeds on wings of vengeance Lanka's impious lord to smite!"

[Bibhishan, Ravan's youngest brother, requested his brother not to fight Rama.]

Anger swelled in Ravan's bosom as he cast his blood-red eye
On Bibhishan calm and fearless, and he spake in accents high:

*"Rather dwell with open foemen or in homes where cobras haunt,
Than with faithless friends who falter and whom fears of danger daunt!*

*O, the love of near relations! — false and faithless,
full of guile, —
How they sorrow at my glory, at my danger how
they smile,
How they grieve with secret anguish when my loftier virtues shine,
How they harbour jealous envy when deserts and
fame are mine,
How they scan with curious vision every fault that
clouds my path,
How they wait with eager longing till I fall in
Fortune's wrath!*

*Rain-drops fall upon the lotus but unmingling hang
apart,
False relations round us gather but they blend not
heart with heart,
Winter clouds are big with thunder but they shed no
freshening rain,
False relations smile and greet us but their soothing
words are vain,
Bees are tempted by the honey but from flower to
flower they range,
False relations share our favour but in secret seek
a change!*

Lying is thy speech, Bibhishan, secret envy lurks
within,
Thou wouldst rule thy elder's empire, thou wouldst
wed thy elder's queen,

Take thy treason to the foemen, — brother's blood I may not shed, —
Other Raksha craven-hearted by my royal hands had bled!"

[Lanka was seiged by Ravan's army. Both parties fought bravely. Both Rama and Lertshan were severely wounded and were about to die. Ravan took his beloved son Indajit and his dear brother Kembhutarna in the war. Ravan himself entered the battle field three times. The third battle of Ravan's was fierce indeed.]

### Ravan's Last Battle and Fall

Gods and mortals watched the contest and the heroes of the war,
Ravan speeding on his chariot, Rama on the heavenly car,

And a fiercer form the warriors in their fiery frenzy wore,
And a deeper weight of hatred on their anguished bosoms bore,

Clouds of dread and deathful arrows hid the radiant face of sky,
Darker grew the day of combat, fiercer grew the contest high!

Pierced by Ravan's pointed weapons bleeding Rama owned no pain,
Rama's arrows keen and piercing sought his foeman's life in vain,

Long the dubious battle lasted, and with wilder fury fraught,
Wounded, faint, and still unyielding, blind with wrath the rivals fought,

Pike and club and mace and trident 'scaped from Ravan's vengeful hand,
Spear and arrows Rama wielded, and his bright and flaming brand!

Long the dubious battle lasted, shook the ocean, hill and dale,
Winds were hushed in voiceless terror and the livid sun was pale,

Still the dubious battle lasted, until Rama in his ire,
Wielded BRAHMA's deathful weapon flaming with celestial fire!

Weapon which the Saint Agastya had unto the hero given,
Winged as lightning dart of INDRA, fatal as the bolt of heaven,

Wrapped in smoke and flaming flashes, speeding from the circled bow,
Pierced the iron heart of Ravan, laid the lifeless hero low,

And a cry of pain and terror from the Raksha ranks arose,
And a shout from joying Vanars as they smote their fleeing foes!

Heavenly flowers in rain descended on the red and gory plain,
And from unseen harps and timbrels rose a soft celestial strain,

And the ocean heaved in gladness, brighter shone the sunlit sky,
Soft and cool the gentle zephyrs through the forest murmured by,

Sweetest scent and fragrant odours wafted from celestial trees,
Fell upon the earth and ocean, rode upon the laden breeze!

Voice of blessing from the bright sky fell on Raghu's valiant son, —
"Champion of the true and righteous! now thy noble task is done!"

## Ordeal by Fire

For she dwelt in Ravan's dwelling, — rumour clouds a woman's fame —
Righteous Rama's brow was clouded, saintly Sita spake in shame:

"Wherefore spake ye not, my Rama, if your bosom doubts my faith,
Dearer than a dark suspicion to a woman were her death!

Wherefore, Rama, with your token came your vassal o'er the wave,

To assist a fallen woman and a tainted wife to save,

Wherefore with your mighty forces crossed the ocean in your pride,
Risked your life in endless combats for a sin-polluted bride?
Hast thou, Rama, all forgotten? — Saintly Janak saw my birth,
Child of harvest-bearing furrow, Sita sprang from Mother Earth,
As a maiden true and stainless unto thee I gave my hand,
As a consort fond and faithful roved with thee from land to land!

But a woman pleadeth vainly when suspicion clouds her name,
Lakshman, if thou lov'st thy sister, light for me the funeral flame,
When the shadow of dishonour darkens o'er a woman's life,
Death alone is friend and refuge of a true and trustful wife,
When a righteous lord and husband turns his cold averted eyes,
Funeral flame dispels suspicion, honour lives when woman dies!"

Dark was Rama's gloomy visage and his lips were firmly sealed,

And his eye betrayed no weakness, word disclosed no thought concealed,

Silent heaved his heart in anguish, silent drooped his tortured head,

Lakshman with a throbbing bosom funeral pyre for Sita made,

And Videha's sinless daughter prayed unto the Gods above,

On her lord and wedded consort cast her dying looks of love!

*"If in act and thought," she uttered, "I am true unto my name,*

*Witness of our sins and virtues, may this Fire protect my fame!*

*If a false and lying scandal brings a faithful woman shame,*

*Witness of our sins and virtues, may this Fire protect my fame!*

*If in life-long loving duty I am free from sin and blame,*

*Witness of our sins and virtues, may this Fire protect my fame!*

Fearless in her faith and valour Sita stepped upon the pyre,

And her form of beauty vanished circled by the clasping fire,

And an anguish shook the people like the ocean tempest-tost,

Old and young and maid and matron wept for Sita true and lost,
For bedecked in golden splendour and in gems and rich attire,
Sita vanished in the red fire of the newly lighted pyre!
*Rishis* and the great *Gandharvas*, Gods who know each secret deed,
Witnessed Sita's high devotion and a woman's lofty creed,
And the earth by ocean girdled with its wealth of teeming life,
Witnessed deed of dauntless duty of a true and stainless wife!

### Virtue Triumphant

SLOW the red flames rolled asunder, God of Fire incarnate came,
Holding in his radiant bosom fair Videha's sinless dame,
Not a curl upon her tresses, not a blossom on her brow,
Not a fibre of her mantle did with tarnished lustre glow!
Witness of our sins and virtues, God of Fire incarnate spake,
Bade the sorrow-stricken Rama back his sinless wife to take:

"Ravan in his impious folly forced from thee thy
  faithful dame,
Guarded by her changeless virtue, Sita still remains the same,

Tempted oft by female Rakshas in the dark and
  dismal wood,
In her woe and in her sadness true to thee hath
  Sita stood,

Courted oft by royal Ravan in the forest far and
  lone,
True to wedded troth and virtue Sita thought of
  thee alone,

Pure is she in thought and action, pure and stainless, true and meek,
I, the witness of all actions, thus my sacred mandate speak!"

Rama's forehead was unclouded and a radiance
  lit his eye,
And his bosom heaved in gladness as he spake in
  accents high:

"Never from the time I saw her in her maiden
  days of youth,
Have I doubted Sita's virtue, Sita's fixed and
  changeless truth,

I have known her ever sinless, — let the world
  her virtue know,
For the God of Fire is witness to her truth and
  changeless vow!

Ravan in his pride and passion conquered not a woman's love,
For the virtuous like the bright fire in their native radiance move,
Ravan in his rage and folly conquered not a faithful wife,
For like ray of sun unsullied is a righteous woman's life,
Be the wide world now a witness, — pure and stainless is my dame,
Rama shall not leave his consort till he leaves his righteous fame!"
In his tears the contrite Rama clasped her in a soft embrace,
And the fond forgiving Sita in his bosom hid her face!

# BHAGARAD GITA–SONG CELESTIAL

*Arjuna Asks, — How Can He Kill Good Men in Battle?*

How can I, in the battle, shoot with shafts
On Bhishma, or on Drona, — O thou Chief! —
Both worshipful, both honourable men?

Better to live on beggar's bread
   With those we love alive,
Than taste their blood in rich feasts spread,
   And guiltily survive!
Ah! were it worse — who knows? — to be
   Victor or vanquished here,
When those confront us angrily
   Whose death leaves living drear?

In pity lost, by doubtings tossed,
   My thoughts — distracted — turn
To Thee, the Guide I reverence most,
   That I may counsel learn:
I know not what would heal the grief
   Burned into soul and sense,
If I were earth's unchallenged chief —
   A god — and these gone hence!

### *Krishna Answers*

Thou grievest where no grief should be! thou
  speak'st
Words lacking wisdom! for the wise in heart
Mourn not for those that live, nor those that die,
Nor I, nor thou, nor any one of these,
Ever was not, nor ever will not be,
For ever and for ever afterwards.
All, that doth live, lives always! To man's frame
As there come infancy and youth and age,
So come there raisings-up and layings-down
Of other and of other life-abodes,
Which the wise know, and fear not.

### The Soul which is not Moved

THE soul that with a strong and constant calm
Takes sorrow and takes joy indifferently,
Lives in the life undying! That which is
Can never cease to be; that which is not
Will not exist. To see this truth of both
Is theirs who part essence from accident,
Substance from shadow. Indestructible,
Learn thou! the life is, spreading life through all;
It cannot anywhere, by any means,
Be anywise diminished, stayed, or changed.

Never the spirit was born; the spirit shall cease
  to be never;
  Never was time it was not; End and Beginning
  are dreams!

Birthless and deathless and changeless remaineth
 the spirit for ever;
Death hath not touched it at all, dead though
 the house of it seems!

>Nay, but as when one layeth
> His worn-out robes away,
>And, taking new ones, sayeth,
> "These will I wear to-day!"
>So putteth by the spirit
> Lightly its garb of flesh,
>And passeth to inherit
> A residence afresh.

### Spiritual Life

I SAY to thee weapons reach not the Life;
Flame burns it not, waters cannot o'erwhelm,
Nor dry winds wither it. Impenetrable,
Unentered, unassailed, unharmed, untouched,
Immortal, all-arriving, stable, sure,
Invisible, ineffable, by word
And thought uncompassed, ever all itself,
Thus is the Soul declared! How wilt thou, then, —
Knowing it so, — grieve when thou shouldst not
 grieve?

How, if thou hearest that the man new-dead
Is, like the man new-born, still living man —
One same, existent Spirit — wilt thou weep?
The end of birth is death; the end of death

KRISHNA PLAYING HIS PIPE

Is birth; this is ordained! and mournest thou,
Chief of the stalwart arm! for what befalls
Which could not otherwise befall? The birth
Of living things comes unperceived; the death
Comes unperceived; between them, beings per-
 ceive:
What is there sorrowful herein, dear Prince?

### Krishna Tells Arjuna not to Shun the Fray

THIS Life within all living things, my Prince!
Hides beyond harm; scorn thou to suffer, then,
For that which cannot suffer. Do thy part!
Be mindful of thy name, and tremble not!
Nought better can betide a martial soul
Than lawful war; happy the warrior
To whom comes joy of battle — comes, as now,
Glorious and fair, unsought; opening for him
A gateway unto Heav'n. But, if thou shunn'st
This honourable field — a Kshattriya —

If, knowing thy duty and thy task, thou bidd'st
Duty and task go by — that shall be sin!
And those to come shall speak thee infamy
From age to age; but infamy is worse
For men of noble blood to bear than death!
The chiefs upon their battle-chariots
Will deem 'twas fear that drove thee from the
 fray.

## Krishna Explains Yoga to Arjuna

HEAR now the deeper teaching of the Yog,
Which holding, understanding, thou shalt burst
Thy Karmabandh, the bondage of wrought deeds.
Here shall no end be hindered, no hope marred,
No loss be feared: yea, a little faith —
Shall save thee from the anguish of thy dread.
Here, Glory of the Kurus! shines one rule —
One steadfast rule — while shifting souls have laws
Many and hard

      Specious, but wrongful deem
The speech of those ill-taught ones who extol
The letter of their Vedas, saying, "This
Is all we have, or need;" being weak at heart
With wants, seekers of Heaven: which comes —
 they say —
As "fruit of good deeds done;" promising men
Much profit in new births for works of faith;
In various rites abounding; following whereon
Large merit shall accrue towards wealth and
 power;
Albeit, who wealth and power do most desire
Least fixity of soul have such, least hold
On heavenly meditation. Much these teach
From Veda, concerning the "three qualities;"

But thou, be free of the "three qualities,"
Free of the "pairs of opposites," and free
From that sad righteousness which calculates

Self-ruled, Arjuna! simple, satisfied!
Look! like as when a tank pours water forth
To suit all needs, so do these Brahmans draw
Text for all wants from tank of Holy Writ.

But thou, want not! ask not! Find full reward
Of doing right in right! Let right deeds be
Thy motive, not the fruit which comes from
   them.
And live in action! Labour! Make thine acts
Thy piety, casting all self aside,
Contemning gain and merit; equable
In good or evil: equability
Is Yôg, is piety!

### Right Thought

Yet, the right act
Is less, far less, than the right-thinking mind.
Seek refuge in thy soul; have there thy heaven!
Scorn them that follow virtue for her gifts!
The mind of pure devotion — even here —
Casts equally aside good deeds and bad,
Passing above them. Unto pure devotion
Devote thyself; with perfect meditation
Comes perfect act, and the right-hearted rise —
More certainly because they seek no gain —
Forth from the bands of body, step by step,
To highest seats of bliss. When thy firm soul
Hath shaken off those tangled oracles
Which ignorantly guide, then shall it soar

To high neglect of what's denied or said,
This way or that way, in doctrinal writ.
Troubled no longer by the priestly lore,
Safe shall it live, and sure; steadfastly bent
On meditation. This is Yôg — and Peace!

                    When one, O Prithâ's Son! —
Abandoning desires which shake the mind —
Finds in his soul full comfort for his soul,
He hath attained the Yôg — that man is such!
In sorrows not dejected, and in joys
Not overjoyed; dwelling outside the stress
Of passion, fear, and anger; fixed in calms
Of lofty contemplation; — such an one
Is Muni, is the Sage, the true Recluse!
He who to none and nowhere overbound
By ties of flesh, takes evil things and good
Neither desponding nor exalting, such
Bears wisdom's plainest mark!

                    Yet may it chance,
O Son of Kunti! that a governed mind
Shall some time feel the sense-storms sweep, and
    wrest
Strong self-control by the roots. Let him regain
His kingdom! let him conquer this, and sit
On Me intent. That man alone is wise
Who keeps the mastery of himself! If one
Ponders on objects of the sense, there springs
Attraction; from attraction grows desire,
Desire flames to fierce passion, passion breeds

Recklessness; then the memory — all betrayed —
Lets noble purpose go, and saps the mind,
Till purpose, mind, and man are all undone.

### Tranquillity

BUT, if one deals with objects of the sense
Not loving and not hating, making them
Serve his free soul, which rests serenely lord,
Lo! such a man comes to tranquillity
And out of that tranquillity shall rise
The end and healing of his earthly pains,
Since the will governed sets the soul at peace.

And like the ocean, day by day receiving
 Floods from all lands, which never overflows;
Its boundary-line not leaping, and not leaving,
 Fed by the rivers, but unswelled by those; —

So is the perfect one! to his soul's ocean
 The world of sense pours streams of witchery,
They leave him as they find, without commotion,
 Taking their tribute, but remaining sea.

### Action and Meditation, the Two Schools of Wisdom

*Arjuna Asks:*

THOU whom all mortals praise, Janârdana!
If meditation be a nobler thing
Than action, wherefore, then, great Keśava!

Dost thou impel me to this dreadful fight?
Now am I by thy doubtful speech disturbed!
Tell me one thing, and tell me certainly;
By what road shall I find the better end?

### Krishna Answers:

I told thee, blameless Lord! there be two paths
Shown to this world; two schools of wisdom.

### First

The Sânkhya's, which doth save in way of works
Prescribed by reason; next, the Yôg, which bids
Attain by meditation, spiritually;
Yet these are one! No man shall 'scape from act
By shunning action; nay, and none shall come
By mere renouncements unto perfectness.
Nay, and no jot of time, at any time,
Rests any actionless; his nature's law
Compels him, even unwilling, into act;
(For thought is act in fancy). He who sits
Suppressing all the instruments of flesh,
Yet in his idle heart thinking on them,
Plays the inept and guilty hypocrite:
But he who, with strong body serving mind,
Gives up his mortal powers to worthy work,
Not seeking gain, Arjuna! such an one
Is honourable.

Do thine allotted task!
Work is more excellent than idleness;
The body's life proceeds not, lacking work.

There is a task of holiness to do,
Unlike world-binding toil, which bindeth not
The faithful soul; such earthly duty do
Free from desire, and thou shalt well perform
Thy heavenly purpose.

                        He that abstains
To help the rolling wheels of this great world,
Glutting his idle sense, lives a lost life,
Shameful and vain. Existing for himself,
Self-concentrated, serving self alone,
No part hath he in aught; nothing achieved,
Nought wrought or unwrought toucheth him; no hope
Of help for all the living things of earth
Depends from him. Therefore, thy task prescribed
With spirit unattached gladly perform,
Since in performance of plain duty man
Mounts to his highest bliss.

### Arjuna Asks:
  Yet tell me, Teacher! by what force doth man
Go to his ill, unwilling; as if one
Pushed him that evil path?

### Krisbna Answers:
                        Kama it is!
Passion it is! born of the Darknesses,
Which pusheth him. Mighty of appetite,
Sinful, and strong is this! — man's enemy!

As smoke blots the white fire, as clinging rust
Mars the bright mirror, as the womb surrounds
The babe unborn, so in the world of things
Foiled, soiled, enclosed in this desire of flesh.
The wise fall, caught in it; the unresting foe
It is of wisdom, wearing countless forms,
Fair but deceitful, subtle as a flame.
Sense, mind, and reason — these, O Kunti's Son!
Are booty for it; in its play with these
It maddens man, beguiling, blinding him.
Therefore, thou noblest child of Bharata!
Govern thy heart! Constrain th'entangled sense!

Resist the false, soft sinfulness which saps
Knowledge and judgment! Yea, the world is
    strong,
But what discerns it stronger, and the mind
Strongest; and high o'er all the ruling Soul.
Wherefore, perceiving Him who reigns supreme,
Put forth full force of Soul in thy own soul!
Fight! vanquish foes and doubts, dear Hero! slay
What haunts thee in fond shapes, and would
    betray.

### Krishna Teaches Action without Desire of Gain

Needs must one rightly meditate those
    three —
Doing, — not doing, — and undoing. Here
Thorny and dark the path is! He who sees

How action may be rest, rest action — he
Is wisest 'mid his kind; he hath the truth!
He doeth well, acting or resting. Freed
In all his works from prickings of desire,
Burned clean in act by the white fire of truth,
The wise call that man wise; and such an one,
Renouncing fruit of deeds, always content.

### The Flame of Knowledge

The sacrifice
Which Knowledge pays is better than great gifts
Offered by wealth, since gifts' worth — O my
  Prince!
Lies in the mind which gives, the will that serves:
And these are gained by reverence, by strong
  search,
By humble heed of those who see the Truth
And teach it. Knowing Truth, thy heart no
  more
Will ache with error, for the Truth shall show
All things subdued to thee, as thou to Me.

The flame of Knowledge wastes works' dross
  away!
There is no purifier like thereto
In all this world, and he who seeketh it
Shall find it — being grown perfect — in himself.
Believing, he receives it when the soul
Masters itself, and cleaves to Truth, and comes —
Possessing knowledge — to the higher peace,

The uttermost repose. But those untaught,
And those without full faith, and those who fear
Are shent; no peace is here or otherwhere,

No hope, nor happiness for whoso doubts.
He that, being self-contained, hath vanquished doubt,
Disparting self from service, soul from works,
Enlightened and emancipate, my Prince!
Works fetter him no more! Cut then atwain
With sword of wisdom, Son of Bharata!
This doubt that binds thy heart-beats! cleave the bond
Born of thy ignorance! Be bold and wise!
Give thyself to the field with me! Arise!

### UNITY OF ACTION AND MEDITATION
#### *Arjuna Asks:*

YET, Krishna! at the one time thou dost laud
Surcease of works, and, at another time,
Service through work. Of these twain plainly tell
Which is the better way?

#### *Krishna Answers:*
To cease from works
Is well, and to do works in holiness
Is well; and both conduct to bliss supreme;
But of these twain the better way is his
Who working piously refraineth not.

'Tis the new scholar talks as they were two,
This Sânkhya and this Yôga: wise men know
Who husbands one plucks golden fruit of both!
The region of high rest which Sânkhyans reach
Yôgins attain. Who sees these twain as one
Sees with clear eyes!

### True Piety

RELIGION is not his who too much fasts
Or too much feasts, nor his who sleeps away
An idle mind; nor his who wears to waste
His strength in vigils. Nay, Arjuna! call
That the true piety which most removes
Earth-aches and ills, where one is moderate
In eating, and in resting, and in sport;
Measured in wish and act· sleeping betimes,
Waking betimes for duty.

### Steadfast a Lamp Burns Sheltered from the Wind

WHEN mind broods placid, soothed with holy wont,
When Self contemplates self, and in itself
Hath comfort; when it knows the nameless joy
Beyond all scope of sense, revealed to soul —
Only to soul! and, knowing, wavers not,
True to the farther Truth; when, holding this,
It deems no other treasure comparable,
But, harboured there, cannot be stirred or shook

By any gravest grief, call that state "peace,"
That happy severance Yôga; call that man
The perfect Yôgin!

### The Soul Supreme

BUT, as often as the heart
Breaks — wild and wavering — from control, so
  oft
Let him re-curb it, let him rein it back
To the soul's governance; for perfect bliss
Grows only in the bosom tranquillised,
The spirit passionless, purged from offence,
Vowed to the Infinite. He who thus vows
His soul to the Supreme Soul, quitting sin,
Passes unhindered to the endless bliss
Of unity with Brahma.

### The Unattaining

*Arjuna Asks:*

AND what road goeth he who, having faith,
Fails, Krishna! in the striving; falling back
From holiness, missing the perfect rule?
Is he not lost, straying from Brahma's light,
Like the vain cloud, which floats 'twixt earth and
  heaven
When lightning splits it, and it vanisheth?
Fain would I hear thee answer me herein,
Since, Krishna! none save thou can clear the
  doubt.

*Krishna Answers:*
He is not lost, thou Son of Prithâ! No!
Nor earth, nor heaven is forfeit, even for him,
Because no heart that holds one right desire
Treadeth the road of loss! He who should fail,
Desiring righteousness, cometh at death
Unto the Region of the Just; dwells there
Measureless years, and being born anew,
Beginneth life again in some fair home
Amid the mild and happy. It may chance
He doth descend into a Yôgin house
On Virtue's breast; but that is rare! Such birth
Is hard to be obtained on this earth, Chief!
So hath he back again what heights of heart
He did achieve, and so he strives anew
To perfectness, with better hope, dear Prince!
For by the old desire he is drawn on
Unwittingly; and only to desire
The purity of Yôg is to pass
Beyond the Sabdabrahm, the spoken Ved.

But, being Yôgi, striving strong and long,
Purged from transgressions, perfected by births
Following on births, he plants his feet at last
Upon the further path. Such an one ranks
Above ascetics, higher than the wise,
Beyond achievers of vast deeds! Be thou
Yôgi Arjuna! and of such believe,
Truest and best is he who worships Me
With inmost soul, stayed on My Mystery!

### Krishna Reveals His Manifestations

Of many thousand mortals, one, perchance,
Striveth for Truth; and of those few that strive —
Nay, and rise high — one only — here and there —
Knoweth Me, as I am, the very Truth.

Earth, water, flame, air, ether, life, and mind,
And individuality — those eight
Make up the showing of Me, Manifest.

These be my lower Nature; learn the higher,
Whereby, thou Valiant One! this Universe
Is, by its principle of life, produced;
Whereby the worlds of visible things are born
As from a Yoni. Know! I am that womb;
I make and I unmake this Universe;
Than me there is no other Master, Prince!

No other Maker! All these hang on me
As hangs a row of pearls upon its string.
I am the fresh taste of the water; I
The silver of the moon, the gold o' the sun,
The word of worship in the Veda, the thrill
That passeth in the ether, and the strength
Of man's shed seed.

                    I am the good sweet smell
Of the moistened earth, I am the fire's red light,
The vital air moving in all which moves,
The holiness of hollowed souls, the root
Undying, whence hath sprung whatever is;

The wisdom of the wise, the intellect
Of the informed, the greatness of the great
The splendour of the splendid.

### Lower Conceptions

THERE be those, too, whose knowledge, turned aside
By this desire or that, gives them to serve
Some lower gods, with various rites, constrained
By that which mouldeth them. Unto all such —
Worship what shrine they will, what shapes, in faith —
'Tis I who give them faith! I am content!
The heart thus asking favour from its God,
Darkened but ardent, hath the end it craves,
The lesser blessing — but 'tis I who give!
Yet soon is withered what small fruit they reap:
Those men of little minds, who worship so,
Go where they worship, passing with their gods.

### The Unmanifested

BUT Mine come unto me! Blind are the eyes
Which deem th' Unmanifested manifest,
Not comprehending Me in my true Self!
Imperishable, viewless, undeclared,
Hidden behind my magic veil of shows,
I am not seen by all; I am not known —
Unborn and changeless — to the idle world.
But I, Arjuna! know all things which were,

And all which are, and all which are to be,
Albeit not one among them knoweth Me!

The minds untaught mistake Me, veiled in
    form; —
Nought see they of My secret Presence, nought
Of My hid Nature, ruling all which lives.
Vain hopes pursuing, vain deeds doing; fed
On vainest knowledge, senselessly they seek
An evil way, the way of brutes and fiends.

### Highest Manifestations

BUT My Mahatmas, those of noble soul
Who tread the path celestial, worship Me
With hearts unwandering, — knowing Me the
    Source,
Th' Eternal Source, of Life. Unendingly
They glorify Me; seek Me; keep their vows
Of reverence and love, with changeless faith
Adoring Me. Yea, and those too adore,
Who, offering sacrifice of wakened hearts,
Have sense of one pervading Spirit's stress,
One Force in every place, though manifold!
I am the Sacrifice! I am the Prayer!
I am the Funeral-Cake set for the dead!
I am the healing herb! I am the ghee,
The Mantra, and the flame, and that which burns!
I am — of all this boundless Universe —
The Father, Mother, Ancestor, and Guard!
The end of Learning! That which purifies

In lustral water! I am OM! I am
Rig-Veda, Sama-Veda, Yajur-Ved;
The Way, the Fosterer, the Lord, the Judge,
The Witness; the Abode, the Refuge-House,
The Friend, the Fountain and the Sea of Life
Which sends, and swallows up; Treasure of
    Worlds
And Treasure-Chamber! Seed and Seed-Sower,
Whence endless harvests spring! Sun's heat is
    mine;
Heaven's rain is mine to grant or to withhold;
Death am I, and Immortal Life I am,
Arjuna! Sat and Asat, — Visible Life,
And Life Invisible!

### Divine Love and Compassion

I AM alike for all! I know not hate,
I know not favour! What is made is Mine!
But them that worship Me with love, I love;
They are in Me, and I in them!

                              Nay, Prince!
If one of evil life turn in his thought
Straightly to Me, count him amidst the good;
He hath the high way chosen; he shall grow
Righteous ere long; he shall attain that peace
Which changes not. Thou Prince of India!

Be certain none can perish, trusting Me!
O Prithâ's Son! whoso will turn to Me!
Though they be born from the very womb of Sin,

Woman or man; sprung of the Vaisya caste
Or lowly disregarded Sudra, — all
Plant foot upon the highest path; how then
The holy Brahmans and My Royal Saints?
Ah! ye who into this ill world are come —
Fleeting and false — set your faith fast on Me!
Fix heart and thought on Me! Adore Me! Bring
Offerings to Me! Make Me prostrations! Make
Me your supremest joy! and, undivided,
Unto My rest your spirits shall be guided.

### True Wisdom

HUMBLENESS, truthfulness, and harmlessness,
Patience and honour, reverence for the wise,
Purity, constancy, control of self,
Contempt of sense-delights, self-sacrifice,
Perception of the certitude of ill
In birth, death, age, disease, suffering, and sin;
Detachment, lightly holding unto home,
Children, and wife, and all that bindeth men;
An ever-tranquil heart in fortunes good
And fortunes evil, with a will set firm
To worship Me — Me only! ceasing not;
Loving all solitudes, and shunning noise
Of foolish crowds; endeavours resolute
To reach perception of the Utmost Soul,
And grace to understand what gain it were
So to attain, — this is true Wisdom, Prince!
And what is otherwise is ignorance!

Whoso thus knows himself, and knows his soul
PURUSHA, working through the qualities
With Nature's modes, the light hath come for him!
Whatever flesh he bears, never again
Shall he take on its load. Some few there be
By meditation find the Soul in Self
Self-schooled; and some by long philosophy
And holy life reach thither; some by works:
Some, never so attaining, hear of light
From other lips, and seize, and cleave to it
Worshipping; yea! and those — to teaching true —
Overpass Death!

### KRISHNA TELLS ARJUNA OF THE SOUL-BINDING QUALITIES

SATTWAN, Rajas, and Tamas, so are named
The qualities of Nature, "Soothfastness,"
"Passion," and "Ignorance." These three bind down
The changeless Spirit in the changeful flesh,
Whereof sweet "Soothfastness," by purity
Living unsullied and enlightened, binds
The sinless Soul to happiness and truth;
And Passion, being kin to appetite,
And breeding impulse and propensity,
Binds the embodied Soul, O Kunti's Son!
By tie of work. But Ignorance, begot
Of Darkness, blinding mortal men, binds down
Their souls to stupor, sloth, and drowsiness.

Yea, Prince of India! Soothfastness binds souls
In pleasant wise to flesh; and Passion binds
By toilsome strain; but Ignorance, which blots
The beams of wisdom, binds the soul to sloth.
Passion and Ignorance, once overcome,
Leave Soothfastness, O Bharata! Where this
With Ignorance are absent, Passion rules;
And Ignorance in hearts not good nor quick. —
When at all gateways of the Body shines
The Lamp of Knowledge, then may one see well
Soothfastness settled in that city reigns
Where longing is, and ardour, and unrest,
Impulse to strive and gain, and avarice,
Those spring from Passion — Prince — engrained; and where
Darkness and dulness, sloth and stupor are,
'Tis Ignorance hath caused them, Kuru Chief!

Moreover, when a soul departeth, fixed
In Soothfastness, it goeth to the place —
Perfect and pure — of those that know all Truth.
If it departeth in set habitude
Of Impulse, it shall pass into the world
Of spirits tied to works; and if it dies
In hardened Ignorance, that blinded soul
Is born anew in some unlighted womb.

The fruit of Soothfastness is true and sweet;
The fruit of lusts is pain and toil; the fruit
Of Ignorance is deeper darkness. Yea!

For Light brings light, and Passion ache to have;
And gloom, bewilderments, and ignorance
Grow forth from Ignorance. Those of the first
Rise ever higher; those of the second mode
Take a mid place; the darkened souls sink back
To lower deeps, loaded with witlessness!

### HE WHO SURMOUNTS THE THREE QUALITIES
*Arjuna Asks:*

Oh, my Lord!
Which be the signs to know him that hath gone
Past the Three Modes? How liveth he? What way
Leadeth him safe beyond the threefold Modes?

*Krishna Answers:*

He who with equanimity surveys
Lustre of goodness, strife of passion, sloth
Of ignorance, not angry if they are,
Not wishful when they are not: he who sits
A sojourner and stranger in their midst
Unruffled, standing off, saying — serene —
When troubles break, "These be the Qualities!"
He unto whom — self-centred — grief and joy
Sound as one word; to whose deep-seeing eyes
The clod, the marble, and the gold are one;
Whose equal heart holds the same gentleness
For lovely and unlovely things, firm-set,
Well-pleased in praise and dispraise; satisfied
With honour or dishonour; unto friends

And unto foes alike in tolerance;
Detached from undertakings, — he is named
Surmounter of the Qualities!

### Spirit Taking on Form

WHEN in this world of manifested life,
The undying Spirit, setting forth from Me,
Taketh on form, it draweth to itself
From Being's storehouse, — which containeth all
Senses and intellect.

The Sovereign Soul
Thus entering the flesh, or quitting it,
Gathers these up, as the wind gathers scents,
Blowing above the flower-beds.  Ear and Eye,
And Touch and Taste, and Smelling, these it
    takes, —
Yea, and a sentient mind; — linking itself
To sense-things so.

### Virtues Leading to Heavenly Birth

FEARLESSNESS, singleness of soul, the will
Always to strive for wisdom; opened hand
And governed appetites; and piety,
And love of lonely study; humbleness,
Uprightness, heed to injure nought which lives,
Truthfulness, slowness unto wrath, a mind
That lightly letteth go what others prize
And equanimity, and charity

Which spieth no man's faults; and tenderness
Towards all that suffer; a contented heart,
Fluttered by no desires; a bearing mild,
Modest, and grave, with manhood nobly mixed,
With patience, fortitude, and purity;
An unrevengeful spirit, never given
To rate itself too high; — such be the signs,
O Indian Prince! of him whose feet are set
On that fair path which leads to heavenly birth!

### The Gift Lovingly Given

THE gift lovingly given, when one shall say
"Now must I gladly give!" when he who takes
Can render nothing back; made in due place,
Due time, and to a meet recipient,
Is gift of Sattwan, fair and profitable.

The gift selfishly given where to receive
Is hoped again, or when some end is sought,
Or where the gift is proffered with a grudge,
This is of Rajas, stained with impulse, ill.

# THE WISDOM OF THE UPANISHADS

## THE REAL SELF

*From the Chhandogya Upanishad*

IT is the Self, free from evil, ageless, deathless, sorrowless, hungerless, thirstless, real of desire, real of purpose. . . . So they who depart without finding here the Self and these real Desires, walk not as they list in any worlds; but they who depart after finding here the Self and these real Desires, walk as they list in all worlds. . . .

These real Desires are covered over by Untruth; real as they are, Untruth is their covering. Man here can see no more any of his folk who depart hence. But when he goes there, into the full consciousness of his selfhood, he finds all — those of his folk who are living, and those who have departed, and whatever else he wins not for seeking. For there those real Desires are that were covered over by Untruth. It is as with men who, knowing not the ground, should walk again and again over a hidden treasure and find it not; even so all creatures, coming to it day by day, find not this Brahma-world, for they are cast back by Untruth. . . .

Now that perfect Peace, rising up from this body, enters into the Supreme Light and issues forth in its own semblance. This is the Self, this is the deathless, the fearless; this is Brahma. . . .

Now the Self is the dyke holding asunder the worlds that they fall not one into another. Over this dyke pass not day and night, nor old age, nor death, nor sorrow, nor good deeds, nor bad deeds. All ills turn away thence; for this Brahma-world is void of ill. Therefore in sooth the blind after passing over this dyke is no more blind, the wounded no more wounded, the sick no more sick. Therefore in sooth even Night after passing over this dyke issues forth as Day; for in this Brahma-world is everlasting light.

### The Infinite I

*From the Chhandogya Upanishad*

"Verily this All is Brahman. It has therein its birth, end, breath; as such one should worship it in stillness.

"Verily man is made of will. As is man's will in this world, such he becomes on going hence; so let him frame the will.

"Made of mind, bodies in breath, shaped in light, real of purpose, ethereal of soul, all-working, all-desiring, all-smelling, all-tasting, grasping this All, speaking naught, heeding naught — this is my Self within my heart, smaller than a rice-corn, or a barley-corn, or a mustard-seed, or a canary-seed, or the pulp of a canary-seed — this is my Self within my heart, greater than earth, greater than sky, greater than heaven, greater than these worlds. All-working, all-desiring, all-smelling, all-tasting, grasping this All, speaking naught, heeding naught — this is my Self within my heart, this is Brahma; to Him shall I win when I go hence. He with whom it is thus has indeed no doubt." Thus spake Sandilya.

### Parables

*From the Chhandogya Upanishad*

"If one should smite upon the root of this great tree, beloved, it would sweat sap, and live. If one should smite upon its midst, it would sweat sap, and live. If one should smite upon its top, it would sweat sap, and live. Instinct with the Live Self, it stands full lush and glad.

"But if the Live One leave one bough, it withers. If it leave another bough, it withers. If it leave a third bough, it withers. If it leave the whole, the whole withers. So know, beloved," said he, "the thing whence the Live One has departed does indeed die; but the Live One dies not. In this subtleness has this All its essence; it is the True; it is the Self; thou art it, Svetaketu."

"Bring from yonder a fig."
"Here it is, my lord."
"Break it."
"It is broken, my lord."
"What seest thou in it?"
"Here are but little seeds, my lord."
"Now break one of them."
"It is broken, my lord."
"What seest thou in it?"
"Naught whatsoever, my lord."

And he said to him: "Of that subtleness which thou canst not behold, beloved, is this great fig-tree made. Have faith, beloved. In this subtleness has this All its essence; it is the True; it is the Self; thou art it, Svetaketu."

"Let my lord teach me further."
"Be it so, beloved," said he.
"Lay this salt in water, and on the morrow draw nigh to me." And he did so. Then he said to him: "Bring me the salt which thou laidst in the water yester eve."

He felt, but found it not; it was as melted away.
"Drink from this end thereof. How is it?"
"It is salty."
"Drink from the midst. How is it?"
"It is salty."
"Drink from yonder end. How is it?"
"It is salty."
"Lay it aside, and draw nigh to me." And he did so.
"It is still present," said he to him; "herein forsooth thou canst not behold Being, beloved, but herein soothly it is. In this subtleness has this All its essence; it is the True; it is the Self; thou art it, Svetaketu."

### The Soul in Sleep
*From the Brihad Upanishad*

"What is the Self?"

"It is the Spirit, made of understanding among the Breaths, the inward light within the heart, that walks abroad, abiding the same, through both worlds. He meditates, as it were; He hovers about, as it were. Turned to sleep, He passes beyond this world, the shapes of death.

"This Spirit at birth enters into the body, and is blent with evils; at death He passes out, and leaves evils.

"Two seats has this Spirit, this and the seat in the world beyond; and midway is a third, the seat of dreams. Standing in this midway seat, He looks upon these two seats, this and the seat in the world beyond. Now as this is a step toward the seat in the world beyond, He makes this step and beholds both evils and delights.

"When He sleeps, He takes matter from this all-containing world, Himself hews it down, Himself builds it up, and sleeps in His own brightness, His own light. Here the Spirit has Self for light.

"Therein are no cars, no car-teams, no roads; but He creates cars, car-teams, roads. Therein are no joys, mirths, merriments; but He creates joys, mirths, merriments. Therein are no pools, lakes, streams; but He creates pools, lakes, streams. For He is the maker. . . .

"When in this dreaming He has wantoned and wandered, and seen good and evil, He hastens back according to His entrance and His place to the bound of waking. He is followed by naught of all that He has seen there; for to this Spirit nothing clings. . . .

"Even as a great fish passes along both banks, on this side and on yonder side, so this Spirit passes along both bounds, the bound of dreaming and the bound of waking.

"But as a falcon or an eagle, when it is wearied with flying about in yonder sky, folds its wings and sets itself to couch down, so this Spirit hastens toward that bound wherein He sleeps desiring no desire, beholding no dream. . . . Whatever waking terror He sees in dreams, when men seem to smite Him or to oppress Him, when an elephant seems to crush Him, or He seems to fall into a ditch, this in His ignorance He deems true. But when like a god, like a king, He thinks "I am this All, universal," this is the highest world for Him.

"This is His shape wherein He is beyond desire, free from ill, fearless. As when a man embraced by his beloved knows naught of whatsoever is without or within, so this Spirit embraced by the Self of Intelligence knows naught of what is without or within. This is His shape wherein desire is won, desire is of Self, desire is not, grief is gone. — Good attaches not, evil attaches not; for then has He overpast all griefs of the heart.

"While He sees not, yet without seeing He sees; the sight of the seer is not to be broken, for it is imperishable. But there is naught beside Him, naught apart from Him, that He should see. . . . When He understands not, yet without understanding He understands; the understanding of the understander is not to be broken, for it is imperishable. But there is naught beside Him, naught apart from Him, that He should understand.

"He is the Brahma-world, O king." Thus did Yajnavalkya teach him. "This is the highest way for Him, this, the highest fortune for Him, this the highest world for Him, this the highest bliss for Him; of this bliss other creatures live on but a morsel."

### THE INWARD RULER

*From the Brihad-aranyaka Upanishad*

HE who, dwelling in the earth, is other than the earth, whom the earth knows not, whose body the earth is, who inwardly rules the earth, is thy Self, the Inward Ruler, the deathless. He who, dwelling in the waters, is other than the waters, whom the waters know not, whose body the waters are, who inwardly rules the waters, is thy Self, the Inward Ruler, the deathless. He who, dwelling in the fire, is other than the fire, whom the fire knows not, whose body the fire is, who inwardly rules the fire, is thy Self, the Inward Ruler, the deathless. He who, dwelling in the sky, is other than the sky, whom the sky knows not, whose body the sky is, who inwardly rules the sky, is thy Self, the Inward Ruler, the deathless. He who, dwelling in the wind, is other than the wind, whom the wind knows not, whose body the wind is, who inwardly rules the wind, is thy Self, the Inward Ruler, the deathless.

He who, dwelling in the heavens, is other than the heavens, whom the heavens know not, whose body the heavens are, who inwardly rules the heavens, is thy Self, the Inward Ruler, the deathless. He who, dwelling in the sun, is other than the sun, whom the sun knows not, whose body the sun is, who inwardly rules the sun, is thy Self, the Inward Ruler, the deathless. He who, dwelling in space, is other than space, whom space knows not, whose body space is, who inwardly rules space, is thy Self, the Inward Ruler, the deathless. He who, dwelling in moon and stars, is other than moon and stars, whom moon and stars know not, whose body moon and stars are, who inwardly rules moon and stars, is thy Self, the Inward Ruler, the deathless. He who, dwelling in the ether, is other than the ether, whom the ether knows not, whose body the ether is, who inwardly rules the ether, is thy Self, the Inward Ruler, the deathless. He who, dwelling in the dark, is other than the dark, whom the dark knows not, whose body the dark is, who inwardly rules the dark, is thy Self, the Inward Ruler, the deathless. He who, dwelling in the light, is other than the light, whom the light knows not, whose body the light is, who inwardly rules the light, is thy Self, the Inward Ruler, the deathless. He who, dwelling in all beings, is other than all beings, whom all beings know not, whose body all beings are, who inwardly rules all beings, is thy Self, the Inward Ruler, the deathless.

Thus as to nature; now as to personality. He who, dwelling in the breath, is other than the breath, whom the breath knows not, whose body the breath is, who inwardly rules the breath, is thy Self, the Inward Ruler, the deathless. He who, dwelling in speech, is other than speech, whom speech knows not, whose body speech is, who inwardly rules speech, is thy Self, the Inward Ruler, the deathless. He who, dwelling in the eye, is other than the eye, whom the eye knows not, whose body the eye is, who inwardly rules the eye, is thy Self, the Inward Ruler, the deathless. He who, dwelling in the ear, is other than the ear, whom the ear knows not, whose body the ear is, who inwardly rules the ear, is thy Self, the Inward Ruler, the deathless. He who, dwelling in the mind, is other than the mind, whom the mind knows not, whose body the mind is, who inwardly rules the mind, is thy Self, the Inward Ruler, the deathless.

He who, dwelling in the understanding, is other than the understanding, whom the understanding knows not, whose body the understanding is, who inwardly rules the understanding, is thy Self, the Inward Ruler, the deathless. He who, dwelling in the seed, is other than the seed, whom the seed knows not, whose body the seed is, who inwardly rules the seed, is thy Self, the Inward Ruler, the deathless. He unseen sees, unheard hears, unthought thinks, uncomprehended comprehends. There is no other than he who sees, no other who hears, no other who thinks, no other who comprehends. He is thy Self, the Inward Ruler, the deathless. All else is fraught with sorrow.

### Light and Darkness

*From the Isavasya Upanisbad*

In the Lord is to be veiled this universe, whatsoever stirs in the world. With renunciation thereof thou mayst enjoy; lust thou after the wealth of none.

Daemoniac are in sooth these worlds, veiled in blind darkness; into them pass after death whatsoever folk slay their own souls.

The One, unstirring, is yet swifter than the mind; the gods cannot reach it as it travels before. Standing, it outspeeds others that run; in it the Wind-spirit lays the waters.

It stirs, and stirs not; it is far, and near. It is within all, and outside all that is.

But he who discerns all creatures in his Self, and his Self in all creatures, has no disquiet thence.

What delusion, what grief can be with him in whom all creatures have become the very self of the thinker discerning their oneness?

He has spread around, a thing bright, bodiless, taking no hurt, sinewless, pure, unsmitten by evil; a sage, wise, encompassing, self-existent, he has duly assigned purposes for all time.

Into blind darkness pass they who worship Ignorance; into still greater dark they who are content with Knowledge.

It is neither what comes by Knowledge, nor what comes by Ignorance; thus have we heard from the sages who taught us this lore.

The face of truth is covered with a golden bowl. O Pushan, remove it, that the keeper of truths may see.

O Pushan, sole seer, O Yama, Sun, child of Praja-pati, part asunder thy rays, mass together thy radiance. I see that fairest shape of thee. Yonder, yonder spirit am I.

The breath to the everlasting wind; and be this body ended in ashes.

Om! remember, O my spirit, remember the work! O Fire, lead us by good ways to riches, thou god who knowest all courses; keep far from us crooked sin, and we will offer to thee exceeding homage and praise.

### Soul

#### *From the Kut'h Upanishad*

The soul is not liable to birth nor to death; neither does it take its origin from any other or from itself; hence it is unborn, eternal without reduction and unchangeable; therefore the soul is not injured by the hurt which the body may receive. If anyone ready to kill another imagines that he can destroy his soul, and the other thinks that his soul shall suffer destruction, they both know nothing, for neither does it kill nor is it killed by another.

The soul is the smallest of the small, and greatest of the great. It resides in the heart of all living creatures. The soul, although without motion, seems to go to farthest space; and though it reside in the body at rest, yet it seems to move everywhere.

No man can acquire a knowledge of the soul without abstaining from evil acts; without having control over the senses and the mind; but man may obtain knowledge of the soul through his knowledge of God.

### The False and the True

#### *From the Chhandogya Upanishad*

"The Self, free from evil, ageless, deathless, sorrowless, hungerless, thirstless, real of desire, real of purpose, this should men inquire after, yea, should seek to know. All worlds he wins and all desires who traces out and understands the Self," said Praja-pati.

Both the gods and the demons marked this. "Come," said they, "let us seek out this Self by seeking out which one wins all worlds and all desires." So Indra of the gods and Virochana of the demons set out on a travel, and without being in compact they both came with faggots in their hands to Praja-pati, and stayed as Brahman-students for two-and-thirty years.

Then said Praja-pati to them, "What would ye, that ye have stayed?"

And they said, "The Self, free from evil, ageless, deathless, sorrowless, hungerless, thirstless, real of desire, real of purpose, this should men inquire after, yea, should seek to know. All worlds he wins and all desires who traces out and understands this Self. This they report to be thy saying, sir; in desire thereof have we stayed."

Then Praja-pati said to them, "The Being who is seen in the eye is the Self" — thus he spake — "this is the deathless, the fearless; this is Brahma."

"Then who is he, sir, that is discerned in water and in a mirror?"

"It is he that is discerned in all these beings. Look upon yourselves in a basin of water," said he, "and tell me what of yourselves you do not perceive."

They looked in a basin of water; and Praja-pati said to them, "What see you?"

"We see in this image the whole of our selves, sir," said they, "even to our hair and nails."

Then Praja-pati said to them, "Put on goodly ornament and fine clothing, attire yourselves, and look in the basin of water."

They put on goodly ornament and fine clothing, attired themselves and looked in the basin of water. Praja-pati said to them, "What see you?"

They said, "Even as we stand here wearing goodly ornament and fine clothing, and attired, sir, so are we there wearing goodly ornament and fine clothing, and attired, sir."

"This is the Self," said he, "this is the deathless, the fearless; this is Brahma."

The twain travelled away content of heart. Gazing after them, Praja-pati said: "They are travelling away, yet have they not found and traced out the Self. They who shall follow this doctrine, be they the gods or the demons, shall be brought low."

Now Virochana came content of heart to the demons, and declared to them this doctrine: "The Self should be gladdened here, the Self should be tended; he that gladdens the Self here and tends the Self gains both this world and that beyond." Therefore it is that here even now men say of one who is not bountiful nor believing nor given to sacrifice, "Fie, a demon!". For this is the doctrine of the demons; and when one has died men furnish his body with food and clothing and ornament, imagining that therewith they will win the world beyond.

But Indra, ere he reached the gods, foresaw this peril. "Even as this Self wears goodly ornament when this body wears goodly ornament, is finely clothed when it is finely clothed, and is attired when it is attired, so likewise this Self becomes blind when this body is blind, lame when it is lame, maimed when it is maimed; yea, it perishes with the perishing of this body. I see no pleasure herein."

He came back, faggots in hand. Praja-pati said to him, "Maghava, as thou didst depart content of heart with Virochana, what wouldst thou, that thou hast come back?"

And he said. "Even as this Self, sir, wears goodly ornament when this body wears goodly ornament, is finely clothed when it is finely clothed, and is attired when it is attired, so likewise this Self becomes blind when this body is blind, lame when it is lame, maimed when it is maimed; yea, it perishes with the perishing of this body. I see no pleasure herein."

"Thus indeed it is, Maghava," said he; "but I will teach thee yet more of it. Stay another two-and-thirty years."

He stayed another two-and-thirty years. Then he said to him: "He who wanders about rejoicing in dreams, is the

Self" — thus he spake — "this is the deathless, the fearless; this is Brahma."

Indra departed content of heart. But ere he reached the gods, he foresaw this peril: "This Self indeed becomes not blind though the body be blind, nor lame though it be lame, nor is it defiled by the defilement thereof; it is not stricken by the smiting thereof, nor is it lamed with the lameness thereof; but nevertheless it is as if it were stricken, as if it were hustled, as if it were feeling unpleasantness, as if it were weeping. I see no pleasure herein."

He came back, faggots in hand. Praja-pati said to him, "Maghava, as thou didst depart content of heart, what wouldst thou, that thou hast come back?"

And he said: "This Self indeed becomes not blind though the body be blind, nor lame though it be lame, nor is it defiled by the defilement thereof; it is not stricken by the smiting thereof, nor is it lamed with the lameness thereof; but nevertheless it is as if it were stricken, as if it were hustled, as if it were feeling unpleasantness, as if it were weeping. I see no pleasure herein."

"Thus indeed it is, Maghava," said he; "but I will teach thee yet more of it. Stay another two-and-thirty years."

He stayed another two-and-thirty years. Then he said to him: "When one sleeps utterly and in perfect peace so that he beholds no dream, this is the Self," — thus he spake — "this is the deathless, the fearless; this is Brahma."

He departed content of heart. But before he reached the gods, he foresaw this peril: "Truly one thus knows no longer himself as 'I am,' nor these creatures. He has sunk into destruction. I see no pleasure herein."

He came back, faggots in hand. Praja-pati said to him, "Maghava, as thou didst depart content of heart, what wouldst thou, that thou hast come back?"

And he said: "Truly, sir, one thus knows no longer himself as 'I am,' nor these creatures. He has sunk into destruction. I see no pleasure herein."

"Thus indeed it is, Maghava," said he; "but I will teach thee yet more of it; it is nowhere but in this. Stay another five years."

He stayed another five years. These amount to one hundred and one years; so men say, "Verily Maghava stayed for one hundred and one years as Brahman-student with Praja-pati." Then he said to him: "Verily, Maghava, this body is mortal, held in the grasp of Death; but it is the seat of this deathless, bodiless self. The Embodied is held in the grasp of joy and sorrow; for what is embodied cannot be quit of joy and sorrow. But joy and sorrow touch not what is unembodied. Unembodied is the wind; unembodied are the cloud, the lightning, the thunder. As these, rising up from yonder ether, pass into the Supreme Light and issue forth each in its own semblance, so likewise this perfect Peace, rising up from this body, passes into the Supreme Light and issues forth in its own semblance. This is the Highest Spirit. . . . Now when the eye is fixed upon the ether, that is the spirit in the eye which sees; the eye is but a means to see. When one thinks that he will smell a thing, it is the Self; the nostril is but a means to smell. When one thinks that he will utter a word, it is the Self; speech is but a means to utterance. When one thinks that he will hear a thing, it is the Self; the ear is but a means to hearing. When one thinks that he will think of a thing, it is the Self; the mind is his divine eye; with this divine eye he sees these desires and rejoices therein. . . . All worlds he wins and all desires who traces out and understands the Self." Thus spake Praja-pati.

### Future Life

*From the Kut'b Upanisbad*

NUCHIKETA said, "Some are of opinion that after man's decease existance continues, and others say it ceases. Hence a doubt has arisen respecting the nature of the soul;

I therefore wish to be instructed by thee in this matter. This is the last of the favours thou hast offered."

Yuma replied, "Even gods have doubted and disputed on this subject, which being obscure can never be thoroughly comprehended. Ask, O Nuchiketa! another favour instead of this. Do not thou take advantage of my promise, but give up this request."

Nuchiketa replied, "I am positively informed that gods entertained doubts on this subject, and even thou, O Yuma! callest it difficult of comprehension. But no instructor on this point equal to thee can be found, and no other object is so desirable as this."

Yuma said, "Do thou rather request of me to give thee sons and grandsons, each to attain the age of a hundred years; numbers of cattle, elephants, gold and horses; also extensive empire on earth where thou shalt live as many years as thou wishest.

"If thou knowest another object equally desirable with these, ask it; together with wealth and long life. Thou mayest reign, O Nuchiketa! over a great kingdom. I will enable thee to enjoy all wished-for objects. Ask according to thy desire all objects that are difficult of acquisition in the mortal world, but do not put to me, O Nuchiketa, the question respecting existence after death."

Nuchiketa then replied, "The acquisitions of the enjoyments thou hast offered, O Yuma! is in the first place doubtful, and should they be obtained, they destroy the strength of all the senses; therefore let thy equipages, and thy dancing and music remain with thee.

"A mortal being, whose habitation is the low mansion of earth, and who is liable to sudden extinction, when he approaches the gods exempted from death and debility and understands from them that there is a knowledge of futurity, should not ask of them any inferior favour, and knowing the fleeting nature of music, sexual gratification and sensual pleasures, who can take delight in a long life on earth? Do thou instruct us in that knowledge which removes doubts respecting existence after death, and which is obscure and acquirable with difficulty. I, Nuchiketa, cannot ask any other favour but this."

## DEVOTION
### From the Munduk-Upanisbad

Two birds — God and the soul — co-habitant and co-essential reside unitedly in one tree, which is the body. One of them, — the soul, — consumes the variously-flavoured fruits of its actions; but the other, — God, — without partaking of them, witnesses all events.

The soul, so pressed down in the body, being deluded with ignorance, grieves at its own insufficiency, but when it perceives its co-habitant, the adorable Lord of the universe, the origin of itself, and His glory, it feels relieved from grief and infatuation. A wise man knowing God as perspicuously residing in all creatures forsakes all idea of duality; being convinced that there is only one real existence, which is God. He then directs all his senses toward God alone, the origin of self-consciousness, and on Him exclusively he places his love, abstracting at the same time his mind from all worldly objects by constantly applying it to God. Through strict veracity, the uniform direction of mind and senses, and through notions acquired from spiritual teachers, as well as by abstinence from sexual indulgence, man should approach God, who full of splendour and perfection works in the heart.

## THE ALL-HIGHEST
### From the Svetasvatara Upanisbad

I KNOW that great Spirit, sun-hued, beyond the darkness. Knowing Him, man escapeth Death; there is no other way to walk.

Than this naught else is higher, nor subtler, nor mightier; with this Spirit the universe is filled.

Formless, sorrowless is the Highest; they become deathless who know it; but others come to very grief.

With face, head, neck everywhere, dwelling in covert in every creature, pervading all, the Lord is He; thus everywhere is the presence of the Gracious.

A great lord is the Spirit, mover of the understanding, ruler of this pure approach, Light unfading.

The Spirit dwells ever as inward soul within men's hearts, conceived by the heart, the imagination, the thought; deathless they become who know this.

Showing himself in the qualities of all senses, void of all senses, He is lord, ruler of all, refuge of all.

Handless and footless, He speeds and seizes; eyeless, He sees; earless, He hears. He knows what may be known, but there is none to know him. Men call Him the Primal, the Great Spirit.

Subtler than the subtle is He, greater than the great, the soul lodged in covert in living beings. Freed from grief, man sees by the Almighty's grace Him, the desireless, Him the Power sovereign.

I know Him, the ageless, ancient, All-soul, dwelling everywhere in universal presence, to whom Brahma-teachers deny birth, whom they call the Eternal.

The one hue that by blending of powers lends manifold hues in diverse wise from gathered substance, the Beginning and End wherein the All dissolves — He is God; may He unite us with blessed understanding!

In vision of the Lord, the bounteous worshipful God, who stands sole warder over every womb, in whom this All falls together and dissolves asunder, man comes to this everlasting peace.

His form is not to be beheld; none sees Him with the eye. Deathless they become who in heart and mind know Him as heart-dwelling.

## Brahma

*From the Later Vedanta*

Always I am, I give light; never am I unbeloved; thus I am proved to be Brahma, consisting in Being, Thought, and Bliss.

In me, the sky of Thought, arises the mirage of the universe; then how can I be aught but Brahma, knowing all, cause of all?

The universe, having no light of its own, could not possibly come to light but for the presence of light; I am the Light, and therefore am everywhere.

I am the Witness, related to all things, most dear; I am never the Ego, for that is plunged in affections, limitations, and pains.

I am the one who knows the beings of change, and am myself changeless; were it not so, I should be altogether incapable of observing their changes.

For a changing thing goes again and again through birth and dissolution in this and that form; how can it be an observer of these changes?

There is apparent in the sky of Thought a certain mist which subsists on the lack of reflections and ends with the rise of the sun of reflection.

In this long-drawn dream of which our world is made, and which arises from the great slumber of Self-ignorance, there appear Heaven, Salvation, and the other phantoms.

This distinction between unconscious and conscious being is imaginarily imposed on me, the conscious Being, — like the distinction between moving and motionless figures in a picture on a level wall.

I, the ocean of ambrosia, decay not because phantom bubbles arise; I, the mountain of crystal, am not flushed by the play of dream-fashioned evening clouds.

No real thing forsooth can ever be of diverse essence;

thus I am without inward distinction, void of the differences arising from the world.

I am the Power self-authoritative and absolute, in which are stilled the phantom figures of the world and separate souls, of disciples and masters.

## VIVEKANANDA ON YOGA PHILOSOPHY

According to Yoga philosophy it is through ignorance that the Soul has been joined with nature and the idea is to get rid of nature's control over us. That is the goal of all religions. Each Soul is potentially divine. The goal is to manifest this Divinity within, by controlling nature, external and internal. Do this either by work, or worship, or psychic control, or philosophy, by one, or more, or all of these — and be free. This is the whole of religion. Doctrines, or dogmas, or rituals, or books, or temples, or forms, are but secondary details. The Yogi tries to reach this goal through psychic control. Until we can free ourselves from nature we are slaves; as she dictates so we must go. The Yogi claims that he who controls mind controls matter also. The internal nature is much higher than the external, and much more difficult to grapple with, much more difficult to control; therefore he who has conquered the internal nature controls the whole universe; it becomes his servant.

Raja Yoga propounds the methods of gaining this control. Higher forces than we know in physical nature will have to be subdued. This body is just the external crust of the mind. They are not two different things; they are just as the oyster and its shell. They are but two aspects of one thing; the internal substance of the oyster is taking up matter from outside, and manufacturing the shell. In the same way these internal fine forces which are called mind take up gross matter from outside, and from that manufacture this external shell or body. If then, we have control of the internal, it is very easy to have control of the external. Then again, these forces are not different. It is not that some forces are physical, and some mental; the physical forces are but the gross manifestations of the fine forces, just as the physical world is but the gross manifestation of the fine world.

# RAMAKRISHNA ON YOGA PHILOSOPHY

THERE are infinite ways which lead to the sea of immortality. The main thing is to fall into that sea; it matters not how one gets there. Suppose there is a reservoir of nectar, a single drop of which falling into the mouth will make one immortal. You may drink of it either by jumping into the reservoir or by slowly walking down along its slope. The result will be the same even if you are pushed or thrown into it by another. Taste a little of that nectar and become immortal.

Innumerable are the paths. Jnâna, Karma, Bhakti are all paths which lead to the same goal. If you have intense longing you will surely reach God. Yoga (communion with God) is of four kinds: Jnâna Yoga, Karma Yoga, Raja Yoga, and Bhakti Yoga.

Jnâna Yoga is communion with God by means of right discrimination and knowledge in its highest sense. The object of a Jnâni is to know and realise the Absolute. He discriminates between the Absolute Reality and the unreal phenomena by saying: "Not this," "Not this," until he comes to a point where all discrimination between the Real and the unreal ceases and the Absolute Brahman is realized in Samâdhi.

Karma Yoga is communion with God by means of work. It is what you are teaching. The performance of duties by householders not for the sake of obtaining their results but for glorifying the Supreme is that which is meant by this method of Yoga. Again, worship, repetition of the Name of the Lord, and other devotional exercises are also included in it, if they are done without attachment to their fruits and for the glorification of God. The end of Karma is the same as the realization of the Impersonal Absolute or the Personal God or both.

Raja Yoga leads to this communion through concentration and meditation. It has eight steps. The first is Yama, which consists in non-injuring, truthfulness, non-covetousness, chastity, and the non-receiving of gifts. The second is Niyama, which includes austerities, forbearance, contentment, faith in the Supreme Being, charity, study, and self-surrender to the Supreme Will. The practice of various physical postures is comprised in Âsana, the third; while Prânâyâma or breathing exercises constitute the fourth step. The fifth is Pratyâhâra and consists in making the mind introspective and one-pointed. Concentration or Dhâranâ is the next; Dhyâna or meditation is the seventh, and Samâdhi or the state of superconsciousness the eighth.

Bhakti Yoga is communion by means of love, devotion, and self-surrender (Bhakti). It is especially adapted to this age.

The path of absolute knowledge is exceedingly difficult. The term of human life at the present day is short and entirely dependent on material food. Moreover, it is almost impossible to get rid of the idea that the soul is one with the body. Now a Jnâni or philosopher may declare: "I am not this body, gross or subtle; I am one with Brahman, the Absolute. I am not subject to the necessities and conditions of the body, — hunger, thirst, birth, death, disease, grief, pleasure, pain." Such assertions, however, will not make him free from these bodily conditions so long as he is on the plane of relativity. He may be compared to a person who is suffering from the intense pain of a wound but who is trying to deny it by mere word of mouth.

When the Kundalini is awakened, true Bhakti, Divine Love and ecstasy are attained. Through Karma Yoga one can easily attain to various psychic powers. But when Karma Yoga leads to Bhakti Yoga, Divine realization comes. Then all duties, rituals, ceremonials, drop off like the petals of a flower when the fruit has grown. When a child is born, the young mother does not discharge any other duties, but fondles the child the whole day. As she is free from all household duties, so a Bhakta becomes free from the bondage of work after realizing God. The true Bhakta says: "O Mother, Karma with attachment I fear, for it proceeds from selfish motives, and as a man soweth so shall he reap. I see again that work without attachment is exceedingly difficult. If I work through attachment I shall forget Thee: therefore I do not desire such Karma. Grant that my work may become less and less so long as I do not attain to Thee. Till then may I have strength to do unattached the little work that is left for me, and may I be blessed with unselfish love and devotion to Thee! Mother, so long as I do not realize Thee may my mind be not attached to new works and new desires! But when Thou wilt command me to work I shall do it not for myself but only for Thee."

' Hatha Yoga deals entirely with the physical body. It describes the methods by which the internal organs can be purified and perfect health can be acquired. It teaches how to conquer the various powers of Prâna and the muscles, organs and nerves of the body. But in Hatha Yoga the mind must always be concentrated on the physical body. A Hatha Yogi possesses many powers, such as the power of levitation; but all these powers are only the manifestations of physical Prâna. There was a juggler who in the midst of his tricks suddenly turned his tongue upward and drew it back into the post-nasal canal, stopping respiration. Instantly all the activities of his body were suspended. People thought that he was dead, so they buried him. For several years he remained buried in that state. In some way the grave was opened and he regained consciousness. Immediately he began to repeat the same conjuring words with which he had been casting the spell before he lost consciousness. So the practice of Hatha Yoga will bring the control over the body, but it will carry one only so far. Raja Yoga, on the contrary, deals with the mind and leads to spiritual results through discrimination, concentration and meditation.

Perfect concentration of the mind is necessary in the path of Raja Yoga. Mind is like the flame of a lamp. When the wind of desire blows, it is restless; when there is no wind, it is steady. The latter is the state of mind in Yoga. Ordinarily the mind is scattered, one portion here, another portion there. It is necessary to collect the scattered mind and direct it towards one point. If you want a whole piece of cloth, you will have to pay the full price for it. Yoga is not possible if there be the least obstacle in the way. If there be a small break in the telegraphic wire, the message will not reach its destination. A Yogi controls his mind, the mind does not control him. When the mind is absolutely concentrated, the breath stops, and the soul enter into Samâdhi.

THE six Lotuses mentioned in the Science of Yoga correspond to the seven mental planes mentioned in the Vedanta. When the mind is immersed in worldliness, it makes its abode in the lowest lotus at the end of the spine. Sexual desires rise when the mind is in the second lotus, the sexual organ. When it is in the third, the navel, the man is taken up with things of the world — eating, drinking, begetting children. In the fourth mental plane the heart of the man is blessed with the Vision of Divine Glory and he cries out: "What is all this! What is all this!" In the fifth plane the mind rests in the throat. The devotee talks only on subjects related to God and grows impatient if any other subject comes up in the course of conversation. In the sixth plane the mind is localized between the eyebrows. The devotee comes face to face with God; only a thin glass-like partition, so to speak, keeps him separate from the Divine Person. To him God is like a light within a lantern, or like a photograph behind a glass frame. He tries to touch the vision, but he cannot. His perception falls short of complete realization, for there is the element of self-consciousness, the sense of "I," kept to a certain extent. In the last or seventh plane it is perfect Samâdhi. Then all sense-consciousness ceases and absolute God-consciousness takes its place.

A RAJA YOGI also seeks to realize the Universal Being. His object is to bring the finite human soul into communion with the infinite Spirit. He tries first to collect his mind, which is scattered in the world of senses, and then seeks to fix it on the Universal Spirit; hence the necessity of meditating on Him in solitude and in a posture which causes no distraction.

WHEN Karma Yoga is so difficult to practice, one should pray to the Lord in this manner: "O Lord! Do Thou reduce our Karma to a minimum, and the little work that we daily perform, may we do it with non-attachment by Thy grace. O Lord! Do not let our desire for work increase in number and bind us to worldliness."

## YOGA APHORISMS OF PATANJALI

SLEEP is that modification of the mind which ensues upon the quitting of all objects by the mind, by reason of all the waking senses and faculties sinking into abeyance.

MEMORY is the not letting go of an object that one has been aware of.

THE meditative state attained by those whose discrimination does not extend to pure spirit, depends upon the phenomenal world.

IN the practice of those who are, or may be, able to discriminate as to pure spirit, their meditation is preceded by Faith, Energy, Intentness (upon a single point), and Discernment, or thorough discrimination of that which is to be known.

THE attainment of the state of abstract meditation is speedy, in the case of the hotly impetuous.

IGNORANCE is the notion that the non-eternal, the impure, the evil and that which is not soul are, severally, eternal, pure, good and soul.

THE tenacious wish for existence upon earth is inherent in all sentient beings, and continues through all incarnations, because it has self-reproductive power. It is felt as well by the wise as the unwise.

BUT to that man who has attained to the perfection of spiritual cultivation, all mundane things are alike vexatious, since the modifications of the mind due to the natural qualities are adverse to the attainment of the highest condition; because, until that is reached, the occupation of any form of body is a hindrance, and anxiety and impressions of various kinds ceaselessly continue.

THE Universe, including the visible and the invisible, the essential nature of which is compounded of purity, action, and rest, and which consists of the elements and the organs of action, exists for the sake of the soul's experience and emancipation.

THE soul is the Perceiver; is assuredly vision itself pure and simple; unmodified; and looks directly upon ideas.

ALTHOUGH the Universe in its objective state has ceased to be, in respect to that man who has attained to the perfection of spiritual cultivation, it has not ceased in respect to all others, because it is common to others besides him.

In order to exclude from the mind questionable things, the mental calling up of those things that are opposite is efficacious for their removal.

When harmlessness and kindness are fully developed in the Yogi (him who has attained to cultivated enlightenment of the soul), there is a complete absence of enmity, both in men and animals, among all that are near to him.

When covetousness is eliminated there comes to the Yogi a knowledge of everything relating to, or that which has taken place in, former states of existence.

From purification of the mind and body there arises in the Yogi a thorough discernment of the cause and nature of the body, whereupon he loses that regard which others have for the bodily form; and he also ceases to feel the desire of, or necessity for, association with his fellow-beings that is common among other men.

From purification of the mind and body also ensue to the Yogi a complete predominance of the quality of goodness, complacency, intentness, subjugation of the senses, and fitness for contemplation and comprehension of the soul as distinct from nature.

By means of this regulation of the breath, the obscuration of the mind resulting from the influence of the body is removed.

Restraint is the accommodation of the senses to the nature of the mind, with an absence on the part of the senses of their sensibility to direct impression from objects.

Fixing the mind on a place, object, or subject is attention.

The continuance of this attention is contemplation.

This contemplation, when it is practiced only in respect to a material subject or object of sense, is meditation.

When this fixedness of attention, contemplation, and meditation are practiced with respect to one object, they together constitute what is called concentration.

When the mind, after becoming fixed upon a single object, has ceased to be concerned in any thought about the condition, qualities, or relations of the thing thought of, but is absolutely fastened upon the object itself, it is then said to be intent upon a single point — a state technically called *Ekagrata.*

A KNOWLEDGE of the occurrences experienced in former incarnations arises in the ascetic from holding before his mind the trains of self-reproductive thought and concentrating himself upon them.

THE nature of the mind of another person becomes known to the ascetic when he concentrates his own mind upon that other person.

BY performing concentration in regard to the properties and essential nature of form, especially that of the human body, the ascetic acquires the power of causing the disappearance of his corporeal frame from the sight of others, because thereby its property of Satwa which exhibits itself as luminousness is disconnected from the spectator's organ of sight.

BY performing concentration in regard to benevolence, tenderness, complacency, and disinterestedness, the ascetic is able to acquire the friendship of whomsoever he may desire.

BY performing concentration with regard to the powers of the elements, or of the animal kingdom, the ascetic is able to manifest those in himself.

By concentrating his mind upon minute, concealed or distant objects in every department of nature, the ascetic acquires thorough knowledge concerning them.

By concentrating his mind upon the sun, a knowledge arises in the ascetic concerning all spheres between the earth and the sun.

By concentrating his mind upon the moon, there arises in the ascetic a knowledge of the fixed stars.

By concentrating his mind upon the polar star, the ascetic is able to know the fixed time and motion of every star in the *Brabmanda* of which this earth is a part.

By concentrating his mind upon the solar plexus, the ascetic acquires a knowledge of the structure of the material body.

By concentrating his mind upon the nerve center in the pit of the throat, the ascetic is able to prevent his body being moved, without any resistant exertion of his muscles.

By concentrating his mind upon the light in the head the ascetic acquires the power of seeing divine beings.

The ascetic can, after long practice, disregard the various aids to concentration hereinbefore recommended for the easier acquirement of knowledge, and will be able to possess any knowledge simply through the desire therefor.

By concentrating his mind upon the true nature of the soul as being entirely distinct from any experiences, and disconnected from all material things, and dissociated from the understanding, a knowledge of the true nature of the soul itself arises in the ascetic.

From the particular kind of concentration last described, there arises in the ascetic, and remains with him at all times, a knowledge concerning all things, whether they be those apprehended through the organs of the body or otherwise presented to his contemplation.

The powers hereinbefore described are liable to become obstacles in the way of perfect concentration, because of the possibility of wonder and pleasure flowing from their exercise, but are not obstacles for the ascetic who is perfect in the practice enjoined.

By concentrating his mind upon the relations between the ear and *Akasa* (the ether), the ascetic acquires the power of hearing all sounds, whether upon the earth or in the ether, and whether far or near.

By concentrating his mind upon the human body, in its relations to air and space, the ascetic is able to change, at will, the polarity of his body, and consequently acquires the power of freeing it from the control of the law of gravitation.

WHEN the ascetic has completely mastered all the influences which the body has upon the inner man, and has laid aside all concern in regard to it, and in no respect is affected by it, the consequence is a removal of all obscurations of the intellect.

THE ascetic acquires complete control over the elements by concentrating his mind upon the five classes of properties in the manifested universe; as, first, those of gross or phenomenal character; second, those of form; third, those of subtle quality; fourth, those susceptible of distinction as to light, action, and inertia; fifth, those having influence in their various degrees for the production of fruits through their effects upon the mind.

FROM the acquirement of such power over the elements there results to the ascetic various perfections, to wit, the power to project his innerself into the smallest atom, to expand his innerself to the size of the largest body, to render his material body light or heavy at will, to give indefinite extension to his astral body or its separate members, to exercise an irresistible will upon the minds of others, to obtain the highest excellence of the material body, and the ability to preserve such excellence when obtained.

THE ascetic acquires complete control over the organs of sense from having performed *Sanyama* (concentration) in regard to perception, the nature of the organs, egoism, the quality of the organs as being in action or at rest, and their power to produce merit or demerit from the connection of the mind with them.

THEREFROM spring up in the ascetic the powers; to move his body from one place to another with the quickness of thought, to extend the operations of his senses beyond the trammels of place or the obstructions of matter, and to alter any natural object from one form to another.

IN the ascetic who has acquired the accurate discriminative knowledge of the truth and of the nature of the soul, there arises a knowledge of all existences in their essential natures and a mastery over them.

IN the ascetic who acquires an indifference even to the last mentioned perfection, through having destroyed the last germs of desire, there comes a state of the soul that is called Isolation.

THE ascetic ought not to form association with celestial beings who may appear before him, nor exhibit wonderment at their appearance, since the result would be a renewal of afflictions of the mind.

THE knowledge that springs from this perfection of discriminative power is called "knowledge that saves from re-birth." It has all things and the nature of all things for its objects, and perceives all that hath been and that is, without limitations of time, place, or circumstances, as if all were in the present and the presence of the contemplator.

WHEN the mind no longer conceives itself to be the knower, or experiencer, and has become one with the soul — the real knower and experiencer, — Isolation takes place and the soul is emancipated.

THE mind is not self-illuminative, because it is an instrument of the soul, is colored and modified by experiences and objects and is cognized by the soul.

THE mind, when united with the soul and fully conversant with knowledge embraces universally all objects.

THE mind, though assuming various forms by reason of innumerable mental deposits, exists for the purpose of the soul's emancipation and operates in co-operation therewith.

# WISDOM OF THE HITOPADESA
## Good Advice
### Wisdom and Vision

Wise men, holding wisdom highest, scorn delights,
  more false than fair;
Daily live as if Death's fingers twined already
  in thy hair!

Truly, richer than all riches, better than the best
  of gain,
Wisdom is; unbound, secure — once won, none
  loseth her again.
Bringing dark things into daylight, solving doubts
  that vex the mind,
Like an open eye is Wisdom — he that hath her
  not is blind.

### Noble Actions

Death, that must come, comes nobly when we
  give
Our wealth, and life, and all to make men live.

### Hospitality

Bar thy door not to the stranger, be he friend
  or be he foe,

For the tree will shade the woodman while his
  axe doth lay it low.

Greeting fair, and room to rest in; fire, and water
  from the well —
Simple gifts — are given freely in the house where
  good men dwell; —

Young, or bent with many winters; rich, or poor,
  whate'er thy guest,
Honour him for thine own honour — better is he
  than the best.

Pity them that crave thy pity; who art thou
  to stint thy hoard,
When the holy moon shines equal on the leper
  and the lord!

When thy gate is roughly fastened, and the asker
  turns away,
Thence he bears thy good deeds with him, and
  his sins on thee doth lay.

In the house the husband ruleth; men the Brahman "master" call;
Agni is the Twice-born's Master — but the guest
  is lord of all.

## The Friend

That friend only is the true friend who abides
  when trouble comes;

That man only is the brave man who can bear
    the battle-drums;
Words are wind; deed proveth promise: he who
    helps at need is kin;
And the leal wife is loving though the husband
    lose or win.
Friend and kinsman — more their meaning than
    the idle-hearted mind;
Many a friend can prove unfriendly, many a
    kinsman less than kind:
He who shares his comrade's portion, be he beggar,
    be he lord,
Comes as truly, comes as duly, to the battle as
    the board —
Stands before the king to succour, follows to the
    pile to sigh —
He is friend, and he is kinsman; less would make
    the name a lie.

## The Fated

Stars gleam, lamps flicker, friends foretell of
    fate;
The fated sees, knows, hears them — all too
    late.

## Noble Hearts

Anger comes to noble natures, but leaves there
    no strife or storm:
Plunge a lighted torch beneath it, and the ocean
    grows not warm.

Noble hearts are golden vases — close the bond true metals make;
Easily the smith may weld them, harder far it is to break.

Evil hearts are earthen vessels — at a touch they crack a-twain,
And what craftsman's ready cunning can unite the shards again?

Good men's friendships may be broken, yet abide they friends at heart;
Snap the stem of Luxmee's lotus, but its fibres will not part.

True Religion! — 'tis not blindly prating what the gurus prate,
But to love, as God hath loved them, all things, be they small or great;

And true bliss is when a sane mind doth a healthy body fill
And true knowledge is the knowing what is good and what is ill.

Poisonous though the tree of life be, two fair blossoms grow thereon:
One, the company of good men; and sweet songs of Poets, one.

Sentences of studied wisdom, naught avail they unapplied;

Though the blind man hold a lantern, yet his footsteps stray aside.

BE not haughty, being wealthy; droop not, having lost thine all;
Fate doth play with mortal fortunes as a girl doth toss her ball.

WORLDLY friendships, fair but fleeting; shadow of the clouds at noon;
Women, youth, new corn, and riches; these be pleasures passing soon.

FOR thy bread be not o'er thoughtful — Heav'n for all hath taken thought;
When the babe is born, the sweet milk to the mother's breast is brought.

HE who gave the swan her silver, and the hawk her plumes of pride,
And his purples to the peacock — He will verily provide.

### BEWARE!

AH! the gleaming, glancing arrows of a lovely woman's eye!
Feathered with her jetty lashes, perilous they pass thee by:
Loosed at venture from the black bows of her arching brow, they part,
All too penetrant and deadly for an undefended heart.

By their own deeds men go downward, by them men mount upward all
Like the diggers of a well, and like the builders of a wall.

Not disparagement nor slander kills the spirit of the brave;
Fling a torch down, upward ever burns the brilliant flame it gave.

Never tires the fire of burning, never wearies death of slaying,
Nor the sea of drinking rivers, nor the bright-eyed of betraying.

With gift, craft, promise, cause thy foe to yield;
When these have failed thee, challenge him a-field.

He is brave whose tongue is silent of the trophies of his sword;
He is great whose quiet bearing marks his greatness well assured.

Grief kills gladness, winter summer, midnight-gloom the light of day,
Kindnesses ingratitude, and pleasant friends drive pain away;
Each ends each, but none of other surer conquerors can be
Than Impolicy of Fortune — of Misfortune Policy.

Whoso trusts, for service rendered, or fair words, an enemy,

Wakes from folly like one falling in his slumber
from a tree.

FELLOW be with kindly foemen, rather than with
friends unkind;
Friend and foeman are distinguished not by title
but by mind.

### THE FOUR CASTES
BRAHMANS for their lore have honour; Kshattriyas
for their bravery;
Vaisyas for their hard-earned treasure; Sudras
for humility.

WEEP not! Life the hired nurse is, holding us a
little space;
Death, the mother who doth take us back into
our proper place.

> LIKE as a plank of drift-wood
>   Tossed on the watery main,
> Another plank encountered,
>   Meets, — touches, — parts again;
> So tossed, and drifting ever,
>   On life's unresting sea,
> Men meet, and greet, and sever,
>   Parting eternally.

HALT, traveller! rest i' the shade: then up and
leave it!
Stay, Soul! take fill of love; nor losing, grieve it!

> EACH beloved object born
> Sets within the heart a thorn
> Bleeding, when it be uptorn.

SEEK not the wild, sad heart! thy passion haunt it;
Play hermit in thy house with heart undaunted;
A governed heart, thinking no thought but good,
Makes crowded houses holy solitude.

AWAY with those that preach to us the washing
    off of sin —
Thine own self is the stream for thee to make
    ablutions in:
In self-restraint it rises pure — flows clear in
    tide of truth,
By widening banks of wisdom, in waves of peace
    and truth,
Bathe there, thou son of Pandu! with reverence
    and rite.
For never yet was water wet could wash the
    spirit white.

## APHORISMS

WHAT is the use of matted locks and a body smeared with ashes? He has divine knowledge and final emancipation whose heart melts with benevolence toward all animated beings.

As there are four ways of assaying gold — by friction, cutting, heating, and hammering, — so there are four ways of examining a man, — by his conversation, disposition, family, and conduct.

I WILL declare in a single hemistich what is dilated on in many books — do not to others what would be disagreeable to yourself.

THE wicked man should be avoided -though adorned with learning; — is not the serpent to be feared though it has a jewel in its head?

THE speech of the magnanimous is like the tooth of an elephant, which is never retracted; but that of the base is like the neck of the tortoise which is continually put forth and drawn back.

WHO is free from self-conceit? The partridge sleeps with its feet upward for fear of the sky falling.

From the impurities of the body there is much to fear because all sins enter into it; therefore let your dwelling be with the fearless and conduct yourselves toward the light of God.

For there neither sword nor poison have power to destroy and sin cannot enter. Ye will live ever as God liveth, and the fire of death will be guarded, as it were, with water.

He that meditateth will naturally be happy because he is wise and suffereth not the passions to spread over his soul. He loveth but one God.
— DADU.

### Character

Though he roam to Concan, no dog will turn into a lion; going to Benares will make no pig an elephant; — and no pilgrimage will make a saint of one whose nature is different. — Vemana.

### Hypocrisy

He who has brought his members under subjection, but sits with foolish mind thinking in his heart of the things of sense, is called a hypocrite.
— Bhagavat-Gita.

### Gratitude

The wise will remember throughout their sevenfold births the love of those who have wiped away the falling tear from their eyes. It is not good to forget a benefit; it is good to forget an injury even in the moment in which it is inflicted.
— Tiruvalluvat.

# APHORISMS
## Niti Sastras or Moral Stanzas

He who feeds us is our father; he who helps us is our brother; he who places his confidence in us is our friend; those whose sentiments accord with ours are our kinsmen.

If a margosa seed be dropped into a beverage composed of sugar, honey, and ghee, the whole of it becomes so bitter, that although milk may rain upon it for a thousand years the mixture will lose nothing of its bitterness. This is symbolical of the wicked, who, however good people may be to them, never lose their natural tendency to do evil.

Beware of becoming attached to any country which is not your own, or of serving any master who is a foreigner; renounce all relatives who are only so nominally; keep nothing which does not belong to you; and leave a *guru* who can do you no good.

If you undertake to do anything which you find to be beyond your powers, give it up at once. If an individual dishonours a whole class, he should be excommunicated; if a single inhabitant causes ruin to a whole village he should be expelled from it; if a village causes the ruin of a district, it should be destroyed; and if a district causes the ruin of the soul, it must be abandoned.

IN the afflictions, misfortunes, and tribulations of life only he who actively helps us is our friend.

JUST as a plant of the forest becomes a friend of the body when by virtue of its medicinal properties it cures an illness which afflicts the body, however different the one may be from the other; similarly, he who renders us services should be considered our friend, however lowly may be his condition and however far he may be separated from us; whereas he who affects to be our friend should, if he attempts to hurt us, be regarded as our enemy.

ONE may render good service to the wicked, yet whatever good one may do to them resembles characters written in water, which are effaced as soon as they are written; but services rendered to good people are like characters engraved on stone, which are never effaced.

ONE should keep oneself five yards distant from a carriage, ten yards from a horse, one hundred yards from an elephant; but the distance one should keep from a wicked man cannot be measured.

IF one ask which is the more dangerous venom, that of a wicked man or that of a serpent, the answer is, that however subtle the poison of a serpent may be, it can at any rate be counteracted by virtue of *mantrams;* but it is beyond all power to save a person from the venom of a wicked man.

To attempt to change the character of a wicked man by being kind to him is like trying to make a hog clean. It is no use to mix water with milk and offer the same to an eagle, for the eagle knows the secret of separating the milk from the water. This is symbolical of the wicked.

THE venom of a scorpion is to be found in its tail, that of a fly in its head, that of a serpent in its fangs; but the venom of a wicked man is to be found in all parts of his body.

A WISE man preserves an equal mind both in adversity and in prosperity. He allows himself neither to be crushed by the former, nor elated by the latter.

AN intelligent man is he who knows when to speak and when to be silent, whose friendship is natural and sincere, and who never undertakes anything beyond his power.

VIRTUE is the best of friends, vice is the worst of enemies, disappointment is the most cruel of illnesses, courage is the support of all.

JUST as the crow is the Pariah among birds, and the ass the Pariah among quadrupeds, so is an angry *sannyasi* the Pariah among penitents; but the vilest of Pariahs is the man who despises his fellows.

JUST as the moon is the light of the night and the sun the light of the day, so are good children the light of their family.

FLIES look for ulcers, kings for war, wicked men for quarrels; but good men look only for peace.

THE virtuous man may be compared to a large leafy tree which, while it is itself exposed to the heat of the sun, gives coolness and comfort to others by covering them with its shade.

WHEN we die the money and jewels which we have taken such trouble to amass during our life remain in the house. Our relatives and friends accompany us only to the funeral pyre where our bodies are burnt; but our virtues and our vices follow us beyond the grave.

TEMPORAL blessings pass like a dream, beauty fades like a flower, the longest life disappears like a flash. Our existence may be likened to the bubble that forms on the surface of water.

TAKE heed not to trust yourself to the current of a river, to the claws or the horns of an animal, or to the promises of kings.

TAKE heed to place no trust in a false friend; only disappointment will be experienced from a wicked woman; nothing good can be hoped for from a person who is forced to act against his inclinations; nothing but misfortune can be looked for in a country where injustice prevails.

A MAN of courage is recognizable in a moment of danger, a good wife when one is reduced to misery, firm friends in time of adversity, and faithful relatives at the time of a marriage.

A HYPOCRITE who disguises his true character and wishes to pass for an honest man is comparable to strong vinegar which one tries to make sweet by mixing with it camphor, musk, and sandal. The attempt may well be made, but the vinegar will never altogether lose its sourness.

To show friendship for a man in his presence and to libel him in his absence is to mix nectar with poison.

A MIRROR is of no use to a blind man; in the same way knowledge is of no use to a man without discernment.

TAKE care to spend nothing without hope of profit; to undertake nothing without reflection; to begin no quarrel without good cause. He who does not follow these golden rules courts his own ruin.

HE who works with diligence will never feel hunger; he who devoutly meditates will never commit any great sin; he who is vigilant will never feel fear; and he who knows when to speak and when to be silent will never be drawn into a quarrel.

TRUTH is our mother, justice our father, pity our wife, respect for others our friend, clemency our children. Surrounded by such relatives we have nothing to fear.

IT is easier to snatch a pearl from the jaws of a crocodile or to twist an angry serpent round one's head, like a garland of flowers, without incurring danger, than to make an ignorant and obstinate person change his ideas.

THE miser acknowledges neither god nor *guru*, neither parents nor friends. He who suffers from hunger pays no heed whether the viands be well or ill seasoned. He who loves and cultivates knowledge has no taste for idleness. The froward person has neither shame nor restraint.

TEMPORAL blessings are like foam upon the water; youth passes like a shadow; riches disappear like clouds before the wind. Therefore to virtue alone should we hold fast.

LET us realize well that death watches like a tiger to seize us unawares, sickness pursues us like a relentless enemy, earthly joys are like a leaky vessel from which water trickles ceaselessly until it is empty.

BEFORE the existence of earth, water, air, wind, fire, Brahma, Vishnu, Siva, sun, stars, and other objects, God One and Eternal was in existence.

PRIDE and arrogance suit no one; constancy, humanity, sweetness, compassion, truth, love for one's neighbour, conjugal fidelity, goodness, amiability, cleanliness are all qualities that distinguish really virtuous people. He who possesses all these ten qualities is a true *guru*.

UNHAPPY is the son whose father contracts debts; unhappy is the father whose son bears a bad character; unhappy is the wife whose husband is unfaithful.

To show friendship to a man while he is prosperous and to turn one's back upon him when he is in distress, is to imitate the conduct of prostitutes, who evince affection for their protectors only so long as they are opulent and abandon them as soon as they are ruined.

THERE are six things which almost invariably entail unhappy consequences — the service of kings, robbery, horsebreaking, the accumulation of wealth, sorcery, and anger.

NEVER make known one's condition, one's wealth, one's mistress, one's *mantrams*, one's remedies, the place where one has hidden his money, the good works which one does, the insults one has received, or the debts which one has contracted.

KNOWLEDGE is the health of the body, poverty is its plague, gaiety is its support, sadness makes it grow old.

A SHAMELESS man fears the maladies engendered by luxury, a man of honour fears contempt, a rich person fears the rapacity of kings, gentleness fears violence, beauty fears old age, the penitent fears the influence of the senses, the body fears Yama, the god of death; but the miser and the envious fear nothing.

JUST as milk nourishes the body and intemperance causes it to sicken, so does meditation nourish the spirit, while dissipation enervates it.

IT is prudent to live on good terms with one's cook, with ballad-mongers, with doctors, with magicians, with the rulers of one's country, with rich people, and with obstinate folk.

BIRDS do not perch on trees where there is no fruit; wild beasts leave the forests when the leaves of the trees have fallen and there is no more shade for them; insects leave plants where there are no longer flowers; leeches leave springs which no longer flow; women leave men who have become old or poverty-stricken; a minister leaves the service of an obstinate king; servants leave a master who has been reduced to poverty. Thus it is that self-interest is the motive of everything in this world.

ONLY the sea knows the depth of the sea, only the firmament knows the expanse of the firmament; the gods alone know the power of the gods.

HOWEVER learned one may be, there is always something more to be learnt; however much in favour one may be with kings, there is always something to fear; however affectionate women may be, it is always necessary to be wary of them.

THE meaning of a dream, the effects of clouds in autumn, the heart of a woman, and the character of kings are beyond the comprehension of anybody.

IT is more easy to discover flowers on the sacred fig-tree, or a white crow, or the imprint of fishes' feet, than to know what a woman has in her heart.

THE quality of gold is known by means of the touchstone; the strength of a bull is known by the weight that it will carry; the character of a man is known by his sayings; but there is no means by which we can know the thoughts of a woman.

PLACE no confidence in a parasite, or in a miser, or in any one who meddles in affairs which do not concern him. Do nothing to damage your friend. Avoid all communications with your friend's wife when he is away.

A PRUDENT man will never divulge his thoughts to another before he knows that other's thoughts.

NOTHING is more seductive and, at the same time, more deceitful than wealth. It is extremely troublesome to acquire, to keep, to spend, and to lose.

COURAGE is the most splendid quality in an elephant; high-spiritedness is the most splendid quality in a horse; the moon is the most beautiful ornament of the night; the sun is the most beautiful ornament of the day; cleanliness is the most beautiful ornament of the house; gentleness in words is the most beautiful ornament of speech; virtuous children are the most beautiful ornaments of families; so too is modesty the most beautiful ornament in a woman, and justice the most beautiful quality in kings.

JUST as rain brings an end to famine, the bearing of children an end to a woman's beauty, an illicit transaction an end to the wealth of him who permits it; so does the degradation into which great people may fall bring an end to their greatness.

WHEN one sees blades of *sabrabi*-grass on white-ant heaps one can tell at once that snakes are there; so when one sees anybody frequenting the company of wicked men one may feel sure that he is as wicked as the others.

GREAT rivers, shady trees, medicinal plants, and virtuous people are not born for themselves, but for the good of mankind in general.

THE joy of a Brahmin invited to a good feast, of a famished cow to which fresh grass is offered, or of a virtuous woman who goes to a feast where she meets her long-absent husband is not greater than that of a good soldier who goes to the wars.

ONLY death can cut short the affection of a faithful woman for her family, of a tiger and other wild animals for their claws, of a miser for his riches, of a warrior for his weapons.

TAKE care not to fix your abode in a place where there is no temple, no headman, no school, no river, no astrologer, and no doctor.

WE may descend into hell, establish our dwelling in the abode of Brahma or in the paradise of Indra, throw ourselves into the depths of the sea, ascend to the summit of the highest mountain, take up our habitation in the howling desert or in the town where Kubera reigns, take refuge with Yama, bury ourselves in the bowels of the earth, brave the dangers of battle, sojourn in the midst of venomous reptiles or take up our abode in the moon; yet our destiny will none the less be accomplished. All that will happen to us will be such as it is not in our power to avoid.

BAD ministers cause the ruin of kings, evil opportunities that of young men, worldly communications that of penitents, good works done without discernment that of Brahmins.

THE vice or virtue which prevails in a kingdom is attributed to the monarch; the faults of kings, to their ministers; the defects of women, to their husbands; those of children, to their parents; and those of disciples, to their *gurus*.

JUST as intoxicating liquors destroy our sense of taste, so does a son of bad character destroy a whole family. The society of wicked men dishonours those whose company they frequent. Self-interest destroys friendships that are most firmly cemented.

HE who boasts of knowing that which he does not know and he who affects not to know that which he does know are equally blameworthy.

THERE are three kinds of persons who are well received everywhere, — a gallant warrior, a learned man, and a pretty woman.

THE favours of a prostitute appear like nectar at first, but they soon become poison.

THE pursuit of knowing is troublesome at first, but knowledge is a source of great delight when it is acquired.

A VIRTUOUS man ought to be like the sandal-tree, which perfumes the axe that destroys it.

## WISDOM OF KAPILA
#### FOUNDER OF THE SANKHYA SYSTEM OF PHILOSOPHY

NOT in a perturbed mind does wisdom spring.

HINDU idea is this, that the lotus wherever it grows is beautiful and pure.

SUCCESS is slow; and not even, though instruction be heard, is the end gained without reflection.

NOT by enjoyment is desire appeased.

GO not, of thine own will, near to one driven by strong desire.

HE who is without hopes is happy.

THOUGH one devote himself to many teachers, he must take the essence, as the bee from the flowers.

LIBERATION obtained through knowledge of the twenty-five principles teaches the one only knowledge, — that neither I am, nor is aught mine, nor do I exist.

SCRIPTURAL rites and forms are but works; they are not the chief end of man.

PAIN to victims must bring pain to the sacrificer of them.

SOUL is other than body; not material, because over-seeing physical nature, and because, while this is the thing experienced, the soul it is that experiences.

ATOMS are not the cause of it, for atoms have neither pleasure nor pain.

LIGHT does not pertain to the unintelligent, and the soul is essential light.

MIND, as product of undiscerning activity and as made of parts, is perishable, but not soul. It is an error to mistake even mind, as such, for soul.

ONLY soul can be liberated; because only that can be isolated, in which blind, changeful qualities are but reflected, and do not constitute its essence.

## KAPILA'S CRITICISMS OF THE BRAHMANS

O FOLK of the world, folk of the world, hearken, hearken, to what I proclaim with beat of the drum of my mouth by the stick of my tongue. The term of man's life is but an hundred years; fifty glide away in sleep, five more are spent in childhood, then thrice five are spent in youth, and now that seventy have passed there remain but thrice ten. Few are these days of joy, few these days of sorrow; thus wealth is like a swollen river, youth like the crumbling bank of a swollen river, life like a tree on the crumbling bank. Then do the one thing, the one that is needed — do good, for good is needed; do it to-day, for to-day it is needed. If ye shall say "to-morrow, to-morrow!" ye know not what is your term of life. Whenever it may be that the Death-god cometh, when he doth come he will have naught of your worship of him, naught of your wealth, naught of your proffers, naught of your kindred. He recketh not whether one be good or poor, whether evil or rich. Fierce of eye, he halteth not for a moment; he taketh away the soul, and will have naught of body. O ye hapless mortals who mourn, is it the spirit or the body that is lost? Do ye aver that the spirit is lost? But ye cannot behold it even to-day apart from the body. Is it the body that is lost? But ye tie that very body hand and foot, like a thief who has stolen, strip it of its clothing, fasten on it a loin-cloth, kindle a high-mounting funeral fire, and burn it until it becometh ash, then ye dip yourselves in the stream, and go away with your folks, grieved in soul. Is this to be called a pretence, or a play?

DOTH the rain in its descent avoid certain men, or doth the wind as it bloweth leave aside certain? Doth the earth refuse to bear their weight, or the sun deny its warmth to certain? Do the four high-born races get their food from the land, and the four base-born races their food from the forest? Fortune and poverty are the fruit of our own deeds, and death is the common lot of all children of earth; one is their race, one their family, one their death, one their birth, one the God whom they revere. To neglect not the sayings spoken by the men of old, to give alms at all times to suppliants, to eschew vice, bloodshed, and theft, to know how to stand on a sure footing in righteousness, to understand That which is neither male nor female, to be gentle of speech, — this is the blameless life. Can birth, instead of worth and virtue, bring good, — fools that ye are?

## Liberation through Nature (Prakriti) Kapila

Nature herself shall deliver man from his pain. Man shall know and discern her truth, — not that she hold him bound in ignorance, — is her purport. Unconscious nature lives and loves, in his desire. As people engage in acts to relieve desires, so nature to liberate soul; generous, seeking no benefit, nature accomplishes the wish of ungrateful Soul. Her evolution goes on "for deliverance of each soul: it is done for another's sake as for self." Here is unity of spirit plucked even from the abysses of speculative analysis, of essential distinction! "Nothing," says Gaudapada, "is, in my opinion, more gentle than Nature (Prakriti), once aware of having been seen, she does not expose herself again to the gaze of soul.

How delicate and genial is this sense of illusion, which makes error vanish from the eyes of truth, as one who knows she should not be seen!

Liberation is not through works, which are transient; nor through the worship of the All, which must be mingled with fancies about the world; nor through the desire of heaven, for that desire is to be shunned. It is not the excision of any special qualities; not possessions, nor magic powers; not going away to any world, since soul is immovable, and does not go away; not conjunction with the rank of gods, which is perishable; not absorption of the part into the whole; not destruction of all; not the void, — nor yet joy; but more and better than all these, to know the difference which separates the undiscerning movement of qualities, or tendencies to goodness, passion, and darkness in the senses and the mind, from free spiritual being, and so "to thirst no more"; a work not of a moment but of that complete concentration and devotion, which has many obstacles.

For the great work of liberation, Nature is but an instrument. She, the really bound, "binds herself seven ways, but becomes liberated in one form only," which is knowledge of the truth of things. All is thus for the ideal life of man. "The soul is the seer, the organs are its instruments." "Creation is for the soul's sake, from Brahma down to a post; till there be liberation thereof."

Nature serves soul like a born slave; creates for its sake, as the cart carries saffron for its master. And sense itself becomes supersensuous through this necessity for mind as the explanation of its phenomena. It is a mistake to suppose that sense is identical with that in which it is seated.

The Veda is not eternal; it is not supernatural nor superhuman; its meaning does not transcend the common intuition. He who understands the secular meanings of words can understand their sense in the Veda. There is no special Bible sense; there is no authority of Scriptures apart from their self-evidence and the fruit of their teaching. They do not proceed from a supreme Person; for since one liberated could not desire to make them, and one unliberated could not have power, no such supreme Man or Lord can have been their author. They are there; a breath of self-existence; a fact in other words, traceable to no special mind. That is all that can be said.

## WISDOM OF VEMANA

HE whose form is universal; who is eternal; who Himself witnesses all that passes in every heart, who exists immutable throughout the universe, and is free from all shadow, is called God. Neither in earth, nor metal, wood or stone, painted walls or images, does that great Spirit dwell so as to be perceived.

WE take a skin, and form it into a pretty puppet; we make it play, and then throw it away. But who can see Him who plays with us?

THOSE who roam to other lands in pilgrimage to find the God that dwells within them are like a shepherd who searches in his flock for the sheep that he has under his arm.

"BENARES! Benares!" they cry, and delight to travel thither. Yet is not the same God here as there? If thy heart be aright, He is there and here also.

KINE are of divers colours, but all milk is alike; the kinds of flowers vary, yet all worship is one; systems of faith are different, but the Deity is one.

IF thy heart become calm as the breezeless firmament and the unruffled waveless deep, changeless and unmoving — this is called Salvation.

WHAT Thou sayest I will say; where Thou dwellest I will remain enrapt; my thoughts shall be like to Thine; and when Thou smilest, I will also smile.

VEMANA has many a scornful and bitter word for the Brahman ritualists and ascetic devotees who set their hopes of salvation upon formal ceremonies:
The solitariness of a dog! the meditations of a crane! the chanting of an ass! the bathing of a frog! Ah, why will ye not try to know your own hearts?

WHAT are you the better for smearing your body with ashes? Your thoughts should be set on God alone; for the rest, an ass can wallow in dirt as well as you.

THE books that are called the Vedas are like courtesans, deluding men, and wholly unfathomable; but the hidden knowledge of God is like an honourable wife.

O YE asses! why do you make balls of food and give them to the crows in the name of your ancestors! how can a dung-eating crow be an ancestor of yours?

He that fasts shall become in his next birth a village pig; he that embraces poverty shall become a beggar; and he that bows to a stone shall become like a lifeless image.

If we carefully observe and examine the universe, we shall see that all castes have equally arisen therein. They all are equal; surely all men are brothers. Why should we constantly revile the Pariah? Are not his flesh and blood the same as our own? And of what caste is He who pervades the Pariah?

Would you kill a miser? no poison in the world is needed. There is another way; ask him for a penny, and he will at once fall down dead.

If you take a dog's tail and put it into a bamboo tube, it will remain straight only for a while; say what you will, a bad man will not lose his crooked disposition.

If you catch a monkey and dress it in a new coat, the hill-apes will all worship it. Thus are the luckless subject to the senseless.

He who says: "I know nothing" is the shrewdest of all. He who says: "I am learning" is a mere talker. He who holds his peace is the wisest and best.

# THE WISDOM OF BHARTRI-HARI
## Fond Desires

I HAVE dug up the earth in the search for treasure: I have smelted ores: I have travelled across the sea: I have with great effort calmed the wrath of kings. I have spent my nights in burial-grounds, and I have striven hard to acquire knowledge of religion; but all my strivings have been fruitless. Desire! wilt thou not leave me?

I HAVE wandered over strange and rugged lands, but without profit. I have freed myself from my pride of family; I have carried out valueless tasks: I have put away my self-respect, and have eaten like a crow in the house of a stranger; but yet, O Desire! thou becomest more and more powerful: always with evil inclinations and never satisfied.

I HAVE endured the abuse of wicked men in the hope of gain; I have smothered my tears and forced myself to laugh, though my heart was sad and weary: I have controlled my feelings, and I have bowed down before fools. O fond Desire, how much further dost thou wish to lead me?

DAY by day a portion of our life glides away from us with the rising and setting of the sun, and we think our business of so much importance that we can pay no attention to flight of time. We perceive that birth, pain, and old age end in death, and yet we are not afraid. We are, so to speak, intoxicated — intoxicated by the want of infatuation.

WHY, O my heart, dost thou try from day to day to secure the good graces of others, and yet all in vain? If thou wert only purified, surely all thy desires would be gratified, and thou wouldst not seek the favours of other men, since inwardly thou wouldst be at rest.

IN our periods of health we are alarmed by the fear of disease; in the pride we take in our family by the fear of a sudden fall; in wealth by the fear of a grasping ruler; in honour, by the fear of degradation; in power by the fear of enemies; in beauty by the fear of old age; in our knowledge of the Scriptures by the fear of controversy; in virtue by the fear of evil; and in our body by the fear of death. Everything on earth gives cause for fear, and the only freedom from fear is to be found in the renunciation of all desire.

THESE lives of ours are as unstable as the drop of water on the lotus leaf, and yet what do we not strive to do for their sake? We sin even when we are brazenly boasting of our own virtues in the presence of those wealthy men whose minds have become petrified by the intoxicating power of riches.

ALL hail to the power of Time! The pleasures of the town, the glories of the monarch with his crowds of courtiers, his ministers who stand respectfully before him, his women with faces as beautiful as the shining moon, the crowds of haughty noblemen, the poets and the writers — all these are carried away on the stream of time and eventually become but a memory.

SHALL we abandon the world, dwell beside the divine river, and lead a life of penance? Or shall we rather seek the society of virtuous women? Or shall we study the multitudinous Scriptures, the poetry of which is even as nectar? We cannot tell what we shall do, for the life of a man endures but the twinkling of an eye.

DESIRE resembles a river; its waters are like men's wishes, blown hither and thither by the waves of passion. Love takes the place of the crocodiles, and the birds that soar over the surface of the stream are like the doubts that beset men's minds. The tree of firmness that grows on the bank is carried away by the flood. The whirlpools of error are difficult to navigate, and the steep banks of the river are like unto the troubles of our life. Thus ascetics who, with purified hearts, have succeeded in crossing the river are possessed with unbounded joy.

ONCE upon a time the days seemed long to me when my heart was sorely wounded through asking favours from the rich, and yet again the days seemed all too short for me when I sought to carry out all my worldly desires and ends. But now as a philosopher I sit on a hard stone in a cave on the mountain-side, and time and again in the course of my meditations I often laugh when I think of my former life.

WHOM may we rightly call the over-lords of the earth: those who pay homage to any man? Those who are content to lie on a hard rock; who live in caves; who make their clothes from the bark of trees; whose only companions are the antelopes; whose food is the tender fruit; whose drink is water from the mountain stream and whose wife is wisdom.

## IN PRAISE OF WISDOM

WHEN it happens that sages, whose words are enriched with beautiful thoughts from the shastras, and who convey their sacred learning to their pupils, are compelled to dwell in poverty, then the princes of whom they are subjects must be accused of foolishness, and these sages, however poor they may be, are the real rulers of the country. If those whose business it is to examine jewels are so careless in their methods as to lower the value of the stones, should we not be right in condemning them?

THE man whose mind is of a low order does not take the slightest trouble to pursue wisdom owing to his fear of the difficulties with which he may meet; and, if he does make any attempt, he stops as soon as he encounters an obstacle. On the other hand, the man of superior mind never ceases to pursue when once he has begun, no matter what hindrances he may meet on the way.

### IN PRAISE OF FIRMNESS

The laws regulating behaviour are indeed difficult to learn, and can hardly be mastered, even by the ascetic. The man who wishes to be respectfully silent is liable to be looked upon as dumb: the man who talks agreeably may be thought too forward. If a man stands near at hand, he may be regarded as troublesome, and if he stands far off, people may call him cold-hearted. The patient man may be branded as timid, and the impetuous man is looked upon as ill-bred.

THE friendships which are formed between good and evil men differ in kind. The friendship of the good man may at the beginning be as faint and dim as the first appearance of the morning light, but it continually increases, while the friendship of the evil man is as great at the beginning as the light of the noonday sun, but it soon dies away like the twilight of the evening.

MEN of firm mind never rest until they have carried out to the end the task they have set themselves to do, just as the gods did not rest until they had gained possession of the nectar: for they were not turned aside from their search by pearls of great price, or by fear of dreadful poison.

A MAN's natural disposition, from which his virtues arise, is his most precious ornament — courtesy of a noble man; gentleness of speech of a hero; calmness of knowledge, and reverence of sacred learning. The highest ornament of wealth is liberality towards worthy objects: the highest ornament of the ascetic is abstinence from wrath: the highest ornament of princes is mercy: and the highest ornament of justice freedom from corruption.

THOSE who are skilful in reading character may be inclined to praise or to blame the constant man; fortune may be kind to him or may neglect him: and he may die to-morrow or not for ten thousand years. But in spite of all this, nothing can make him turn aside from the path of righteousness.

Deer, fish and men of virtue, who have need only of grass, water and peace in this world, are deliberately pursued by huntsmen, fishermen, and envious people.

## Destiny

The wealth that the Creator has assigned to him in the writing on his forehead, be it small or great, a man will assuredly find even in a desert, and not more than this will he find on Mount Meru. Then be brave, and live not a life of vanity and misery among the wealthy; see, the pitcher draws the same quantity of water in the well and in the ocean.

## Associations

The water-drop lying on heated iron is known no more, even as to its name; the same, when it lies on the leaf in the lotus-bed, shines in the semblance of a pearl; when it falls into an oyster-shell in the ocean of Arcturus, it becomes a real pearl. The characters of base, commonplace, and noble men are as a rule made by their associations.

## What Profit?

What profit Scriptures, law-books, reading of pious stories, bulky tomes of lore, and the medley of works and rites that win for reward lodging in a hut in Paradise? Save the entrance into the abode of bliss in the soul, which is like Time's fire sweeping away the works that burden life with sorrow, all is but trafficker's craft.

O mother Earth, father Wind, friend Sunshine, kinsman Water, brother Sky, for the last time I clasp my hands in reverence before you. The might of all error is overthrown in me by the stainless radiant knowledge from the rich store of good works born of your comradeship, and I sink into the Supernal Spirit.

# WISDOM OF TULSI-DAS
### THE INCARNATION OF RĀMA

Is there any whom success has not paralysed? who has effectually discarded vanity and pride; whom the fever of youth has not overcome? whose glory has not been ruined by self-conceit; whom envy has not besmirched; whom the blast of sorrow has not shaken, whom the serpent of care has not bitten, or whom delusion has not affected? Is there any so well seasoned of frame that he has not been attacked by desire as a plank by the weevil? The desire of family, of wealth and of renown, is a threefold temptation; whose soul has it not sullied? These all are Mayā's suite; (illusion) — who can describe in full her illimitable might?

Since Siva and Brahma stand in awe of her, why speak of other creatures? Mayā's formidable army is spread over the whole world; Love and the other Passions are her generals, Fraud, Deceit and Heresy her champions. . . . This Mayā, that sets the whole world a-dancing and whose actions no one can understand, is herself set dancing with all her troupe like an actress on the stage, by the play of the Lord's eyebrows. For Rāma is the totality of existence, knowledge, and bliss . . . the Lord that indwelleth in every heart; the Supreme Spirit, effortless, passionless, imperishable; in Him delusion finds no sphere; does darkness attack the sun? For the sake of his faithful people the very god, our lord Rāma, has become incarnate as a king, and for our supreme sanctification has lived, as it were, the life of any ordinary man. As an actor in the course of his performance assumes a variety of dresses and exhibits different characters, but himself remains the same, such is Rāma's divertissement, a bewilderment to the demons, but a delight to the faithful. Sensual libertines in their dulness of soul impute the delusion to the Lord, like as when a man whose eyesight is in fault says that the moon is of a yellow colour. . . .

RĀMA alone is absolute Intelligence; every creature, animate or inanimate, is subject to Mayā. If all had the same perfect intelligence, tell me what would be the difference between God and His creatures? The creature in his pride is subjected to Mayā. Mayā with all its phenomena is subject to God. The creature is dependent on others, the Deity is self-dependent; the creature is manifold, Rāma is one. Though the distinctions made by Mayā are false, without Hari's help they cannot be dispersed, whatever you may do. The wisest of men, who hopes for salvation without prayer to Rāma, is like a beast without tail and horns. Though sixteen full moons were to rise and all the starry host and the forests on every mountain were set on fire, night would not yield except to the sun. In like manner, without prayer to Hari the troubles incident to existence cannot be dispersed. Ignorance has no power over a servant of Hari; knowledge emanating from the Lord pervades his whole being. Therefore there is no destruction for a believer.

## WISDOM OF TUKA-RAM

HE who calleth the stricken and heavily burdened his own is the man of God; truly the Lord must abide with him.

HE that taketh the unprotected to his heart and doeth to a servant the same kindness as to his own children, is assuredly the image of God.

IT is not hard to win salvation, for it may readily be found in the bundle on our back. If we will to have the delights of Faith, our desire shall be fulfilled. Thou, O God, givest to each his fit and meet portion; and I, acknowledging it to be good, gladly receive it. Thou mayst give me the world, as thou wilt; but give me a home for my love.

IF thou lookest on the wife of thy neighbour as on thy mother, what loss is there? If thou chidest not thy neighbours and covetest not their riches, prithee doth it hurt thee? If thou utterest Rāma's name when thou sittest down, what toil is it? No other labours are needed for the winning of God.

WORSHIP with a clean and lowly heart, keep a charitable spirit, do kindness according to your powers — this is the easy way to heaven.

WHERE wilt Thou hide Thyself, my God, when I claim my portion? The Holy Ones bear witness to Thy promise; they know these tokens. I will be as a creditor sitting at Thy door, and will not let Thee come in.

I TAKE refuge with Thee, O God, with all my soul, in body, speech and thought. Naught else hath entrance into my mind; my desire is ever set upon Thee. A heavy burden do I bear; who can lift it save Thee, my God? I am Thy slave, Thou art my Lord; I have followed Thee from afar. I have made a distraint for debt; let us meet for the payment of my reckoning.

IT is needless to lay a child in the mother's arms; she draweth it towards her by her own instinct. Wherefore should I take thought? He that hath the charge will bear the burden. Take no thought for thy body; the Mother will not suffer the child to be harmed.

I HAVE borne toil in order that my last day may be sweet; and now I have won assured repose. The unrest of desire is stilled within me. I rejoice in the outlay that I have made; by it I have gained good fortune. I have wedded the bride Salvation; now shall there be a four days revel.

### The Sikh Morning Prayer

The True One was in the beginning; the True One was in the primal age.
The True One is now also, the True One also shall be.

By thinking I cannot obtain a conception of Him, even though I think hundreds of thousands of times.
Even though I be silent and keep my attention firmly fixed on Him, I cannot preserve silence.
Hungry for God, my hunger ceaseth not though I obtain the load of the worlds.
If man should have thousands and hundreds of thousands of devices, even one would not assist him in obtaining God.
How shall man become true before God? How shall the veil of falsehood be rent?
By walking, according to the will of the Commander as preordained.
He is not established, nor is He created.
The pure one existeth by Himself.
They who worshipped Him have obtained honour.
Sing the praises of Him, who is the Treasure of excellences.
Sing and hear and put His love in your hearts.
Thus shall your sorrows be removed, and you shall be absorbed in Him who is the abode of happiness.

If I knew Him, should I not describe Him? He cannot be described by words.
There is but one Bestower on all living beings; may I not forget Him!

Praisers praise God, but have not acquired a knowledge of Him,
As rivers and streams fall into the sea, but know not its extent.
Kings and emperors who possess oceans and mountains of property and wealth
Are not equal to the worm which forgetteth not God in its heart.

Make contentment thine earrings, modesty and self-respect thy valet, meditation the ashes to smear on thy body.
Make thy body, which is only a morsel for death, thy beggar's coat, and faith thy rule of life and thy staff.
Make the conquest of thy heart the conquest of the world.
Hail! Hail! to Him,
The primal, the pure, without beginning, the indestructible, the same in every age!

## In Praise of Vishnu

### *Rāmānuja*

VISHNU, the Lord of Fortune, whose essence is absolute negation of all evil, accordance with blessedness, and infinitude of knowledge and bliss — who is an ocean of multitudes of boundless and blest qualities of nature, to wit, transcendent knowledge, strength, majesty, vigour, power, and brilliance — whose divine form is a mine of splendour, beauty, comeliness, youth, and other boundless qualities accordant with His will, uniform, inconceivable, godlike, marvellous, constant, flawless, and unsurpassed . . . whose feet are everlastingly praised by countless saints accordant with His will in their essence, being, and activities, delighting solely in doing all service to Him, and possessing multitudes of infinite attributes, such as eternal, flawless, and unsurpassed knowledge, power, and empire — whose dwelling is in the supreme heaven called The Imperishable, which is indefinable by speech or thought accordant with His nature, diverse, various, boundless, abundant in objects, means, and seats of delight, infinite in wondrousness, in splendour, and in extent, everlasting and flawless — whose sport is the origination, maintenance and dissolution of the whole universe, full of endless diverse curious objects of enjoyment and multitudes of enjoyers — who is the Supreme Brahma, Supreme Spirit, and Nârâyana, — after having created the universe from Brahma down to stocks and stones, withdrew into His own nature, and thus became impervious to the meditations and worship of the gods, from Brahma downwards, and of mankind.

But as He is a great ocean of boundless grace,

kindness, love, and generosity, He assumed various similar forms without putting away His own essential godlike nature, and time after time incarnated Himself in the several worlds, granting to His worshippers rewards according to their desires, namely religion, riches, earthly love, and salvation, and descending not only with the purpose of relieving the burden of earth, but also to be accessible to men even such as we are, so revealing Himself in the world as to be visible to the sight of all, and doing such other marvellous deeds as to ravish the hearts and eyes of all beings high and low.

## Purity of Heart

### *Paramananda*

EVERYTHING is conquered by the strength of a pure, unselfish character. When you have purity and unselfishness, nothing more is necessary to bring wisdom. There is naught else in this universe which can give more quickly peace and light to the soul than purity of body and thought; as also there is nothing more potent than impurity to bring the gloom of unhappiness over the soul. This has always been the same. It is the inevitable law. Truth is one and unchangeable. It needs boldness to realize It, worship It and stand by It. Know this and be irresistible with the spirit of Truth and purity.

Know that in the long run Truth must succeed; it cannot be otherwise. Divine Mother's will is going to guide and not the human. Let people exercise their powers and have their experience. But those who are pure in heart, they alone will see the Divine glory. There is nothing like purity; its power is wonderful. Through it one gets almost unlimited vision. But it is very hard to gain. Always value this rare jewel and guard it with all your might. But this is only possible for one who prays constantly to the Supreme Being and has obtained His mercy. Pray with humility and sincerity of heart, then you will never fail.

Remember always that purity and self-control are the greatest treasures in life. Unless you have perfect control over the senses and purity of heart you cannot progress in the path of spirituality. But when you have these, nothing can hurt you or resist you. Always be watchful and pray to the Divine Mother to keep you spotless from all worldliness and egotism. Look to Her for help and guidance. She will make you strong and pure and inspire you more and more with Her Power. So long as Her love and blessings surround you you are safe.

Self-control is gained through the practice of non-attachment. Attachment is a habit and can be overcome by forming a new habit. Hundreds of times you may fail, but you know that unless you learn control you cannot have peace. So practice needs patience. You must struggle continually until you become perfect. You must start just where you are standing now. You must not complain but begin where you are and move onward and onward. Even though you fail thousands of times, you must still struggle to overcome those desires and passions which disturb the lake of your mind and do not let you see your Divine Self at the bottom. Do not think that when you fail, all that you have gained is lost. No; each time you rise after failure, you acquire fresh strength.

Do not be in a hurry; all that you have within will manifest itself in time. Work in moderation. Moderation is the only way to gain health, happiness and peace. When you observe this, then all your efforts will be crowned with success.

## THE WISDOM OF VIVEKANANDA

BE brave and sincere; then follow any path with devotion and you must reach the Whole.

ONE-SIDEDNESS is the bane of the world. The more sides you can develop, the more souls you have and you can see the universe through all souls.

INDIVIDUALITY is my motto. I have no ambition beyond training individuals. I know very little; that little I teach without reserve; where I am ignorant I confess it as such; I am a Sannyasin. As such I hold myself as a servant, not as a Master in this world.

KNOW you are the Infinite, then fear must die. Say ever "I and my Father are one."

UNTIL you are ready to change any minute you can never see the truth; but you must hold fast and be steady in the search for truth.

MATERIALISM says, "The voice of freedom is a delusion." Idealism says, "The voice that tells of bondage is delusion." Vedanta says, "You are free and not free at the same time;

never free on the earthly plane, but ever free on the spiritual. Be beyond both freedom and bondage."

THE greatest sin is to think yourself weak. No one is greater; realize you are Brahman. Nothing has power except what you give it. We are beyond the sun, the stars, the universe. Teach the Godhood of man. Deny evil, create none. Stand up and say, "I am the master, the master of all." We forge the chain and we alone can break it.

THE whole secret of existence is to have no fear. Never fear what will become of you, depend on no one. Only the moment you reject all help are you free.

PHILOSOPHY in India means that through which we see God, the *rationale* of religion; so no Hindu would ever ask for a link between religion and Philosophy.

No law can make you free, you *are* free. Nothing can give you freedom, if you have it not already. The Atman is self-illumined. Cause and effect do not reach there, and this disembodiedness is freedom. Beyond what was, or is, or is to be, is Brahman. As an effect, freedom would have no value: it would be a compound, and as such would contain the seeds of bondage. It is the one real factor, not to be attained, but the rea[l] nature of the soul.

UNCHASTE imagination is as bad as unchaste action. Controlled desire leads to the highest result. Transform the sexual energy into spiritual energy, but do not emasculate, because that is throwing away the power. The stronger this force, the more can be done with it.

NEITHER seek nor avoid, take what comes It is liberty to be affected by nothing; do not merely endure, be unattached. Remember the story of the bull. A mosquito sat long on the horn of a certain bull; then his conscience troubled him and he said: "Mr. Bull, I have been sitting here a long time, perhaps I annoy you. I am sorry, I will go away." But the bull replied "Oh, no, not at all! Bring your whole family and live on my horn; what can you do to me?"

THOSE who give themselves up to the Lord do more for the world than all the so-called workers. One man who has purified himself thoroughly accomplishes more than a regiment of preachers Out of purity and silence comes the word o[f] power.

Go into your own room and get the Upanishad[s] out of your Self. You are the greatest book that

TRIMŪRTI SCULPTURE, ELEPHANTA

ever was or ever will be, the infinite depositary of all that is. Until the inner teacher opens, all outside teaching is in vain. It must lead to the opening of the book of the heart to have any value.

THE will is the "still small voice," the real ruler, . . . The will can be made strong in thousands of ways; every way is a kind of Yoga, but the systematised Yoga accomplishes the work more quickly. Bhakti, Karma, Raja and Jnana Yoga get over the ground more effectively. Put on all head of steam, and reach the goal. The sooner, the better.

NEVER forget the glory of human nature. We are the greatest God that ever was or ever will be. Christs and Buddhas are but waves on the boundless ocean which *I am*.

THE wicked pay the price of the great soul's holiness. Think of that when you see a wicked man. Just as the poor man's labour pays for the rich man's luxury, so is it in the spiritual world. The terrible degradation of the masses in India is the price Nature pays for the production of great souls like Mirabai, Buddha, etc.

THE old idea was, "Develop one idea at the expense of all the rest." The modern way is, "Harmonious development."

TAKE everyone where he stands and push him forward. Religious teaching must always be constructive, not destructive.

EACH tendency shows the life-work of the past, the line or radius along which that man must move. All radii lead to the center. Never attempt to disturb anyone's tendencies; to do that puts back both teacher and taught. When you teach Jnanam, you must become a Jnani and stand mentally exactly where the taught stands. Similarly in every other Yoga. Develop every other faculty as if it were the only one possessed; this is the secret of so-called harmonious development. That is, get extensity with intensity, but not at its expense.

THE true teacher is one who can throw his whole force into the tendency of the taught.

CLEANSE the mind, this is all of religion; . . . The baby sees no sin; he has not yet the measure of it in himself. Get rid of the defects within yourself and you will not be able to see any without. A baby sees robbery done and it means nothing to him. Once you find the hidden object in a puzzle picture, you see it ever more; so when once you are free and stainless, you see only freedom and purity in the world around. That moment all the knots of the heart are cut asunder, all crooked places are made straight and this world vanishes as a dream. And when we awake, we wonder how we ever came to dream such trash.

WITH the axe of knowledge cut the wheels asunder and the Atman stands free, even though the old momentum carries on the wheel of mind and body. The wheel can now only go straight, can only do good. If that body does anything bad, know that the man lies if he makes that claim. But it is only when the wheels have got a good straight motion that the axe can be applied. All purifying action deals conscious or unconscious blows on delusion. To call another a sinner is the worst thing you can do. Good action done even ignorantly helps us to break the bondage.

To identify the sun with the spots on the object glass is the fundamental error. Know the sun, the "I," to be ever unaffected by anything and devote yourself to cleansing the spots. Man is the greatest being that can ever be. The highest worship there is, is to worship man, as Krishna, Buddha, Christ. What you want, you create. Get rid of desire.

WHAT you only grasp intellectually may be overthrown by a new argument, but what you realize is yours forever. Talking, talking religion is but little good. Put God behind everything, man, animal, food, work; make this a habit.

# WISDOM OF ABBEDANANDA
## Human Affection and Divine Love

It is true that human nature seeks companionship and longs for a suitable match for love; but all mortal companions on this plane are only for the time being. That craving of the soul will not be absolutely satisfied until the Eternal object of love is discovered. The Eternal object of love can be realized in the finite and concrete man or woman when we rise above the physical plane and understand that each individual soul is divine and immortal. It is a mere self-delusion to seek the fulness of love in any man or woman. Therefore it is necessary to make the Eternal Ideal the object of all human affection.

Father's love should recognize that Ideal as his child. Mother's love should see it in her newborn babe; the love of a brother or of a sister should establish fraternal relation with It. A husband who is devoted to his wife should think of his Eternal Ideal in the soul of his wife; and a wife should put her highest spiritual Ideal in the soul of her beloved husband and love him with her whole heart and soul. The love of a friend should look upon It as his dearest friend and the

Divine Companion. In this way all earthly relations could be spiritualized and all human affection could in course of time be transformed into the expressions of Divine Love in daily life. There would be no more cause of dissatisfaction in a household, no more fighting between brothers and sisters, no more divorce on account of incompatibility of temper. Then each of these human affections will be like a path that leads to Divine Reality and eternal happiness. Each human affection will then find its right mark the eternal Father, divine Mother, divine child, divine husband and divine friend; since Vedanta teaches that Divinity dwells in each individual soul and can be realized through any of these relations.

In India a true and sincere seeker after Divine Love personifies his Divine Ideal in the form of an Incarnation of God whom he worships as his Divine Master, and loves Him with his whole heart and soul, establishing all relations which are needed in human affection. He says: "O Lord, Thou art my mother, father, friend and relative; Thou art my knowledge and wealth; Thou art my all in all." A true lover of God thus forgets all earthly relations and enters into the holy spiritual family of his divine master. This is the spiritual birth of the soul. If absolute sincerity and earnestness be at the bottom of his heart, and if his love be truly unselfish, then the disciple through this devotion will eventually reach the supreme goal of Divine Love.

The stream of human affection breaking down all the barriers of blood relation and the mountain of selfishness, falls in that river of Divine Love which is constantly flowing from the pure heart and unselfish soul of his spiritual master, into the infinite ocean of Divinity. Thus the true disciple and the divine Master become one in spirit and reach the goal together. In this sense a true spiritual master or divine Incarnation may be called the Mediator, the Saviour of such individual souls who are earnest and sincere seekers after spirituality and Divine Love. This is the path of love for those who are fortunate enough to find such an all-absorbing spiritual Ideal or Divine Incarnation in a human form. Blessed are they who have become the disciples of a Divine Master.

In each individual heart is flowing a stream of love, which like a confined river constantly seeks an outlet through which it can run into that ocean of Divine Love which is called God. It may not find any outlet for many years, or it may remain bottled up for ages within the narrow limits of animal self, but it never loses that innate tendency to run towards the infinite ocean of love. It must find its way out of that limitation sooner or later. Every drop of that stream of love which flows in a human heart, however, contains the germ of Divine Love. As a drop of water in a river contains all the chemical properties of the water of the ocean, so a drop of love, whether pure or impure, is of the same nature as a drop from the ocean of Divine Love. It varies in its character according to the direction towards which it flows and to the nature by which it is governed. When it flows towards one's own self it is animal; when towards another for mutual benefit or for earthly return, it is worldly and human; but when it is directed towards the divine Ideal it is divine.

Divine Love brings a cessation of all sorrow, suffering and pain; it lifts the soul above all bondage; breaks the fetters of selfish attachment and worldliness. All selfishness vanishes and the soul enters into the abode of absolute freedom and everlasting happiness.

The object of attachment in human affection is a changeable and mortal object. While the object of attachment in Divine Love is the unchangeable and Immortal Being, the Lord of the universe.

Some people have an erroneous notion that the Religion of Vedanta teaches that we should not encourage human affection and human love. On the contrary, Vedanta teaches that our life on the human plane will be bitter and dry like a desert if it be not sweetened by human love. If the dew drops of human affection do not moisten the dry and barren heart of a selfish man, how can the germ of Divine Love which is latent in each soul, sprout and grow into a big tree bearing the blossoms of kindness, sympathy, fellow compassion and all other tender feelings which produce the fruits of peace, freedom and happiness! So long as we are on the human plane we should cultivate and practice human love and human affection. But when the soul learns by bitter experience that the object of human love and affection is only an ordinary mortal, when it longs for an immortal something which is higher and greater, when the soul rises from the human to the spiritual plane, and obtains glimpses of that which is unchangeable and absolute; how can such a soul be satisfied with human limitations and human imperfections! It is then that the soul longs for the expression of all affection on the spiritual plane. It is then that the soul becomes a seeker after the Absolute and a lover of the Divine Ideal. Until that time has arrived, one does not care for anything that is higher than human affection. As on the human plane, forced love is never sweet and genuine, so on the spiritual plane love for the Spiritual Ideal or Divine Master must be spontaneous and intense, unwavering and whole-souled; otherwise dissatisfaction and unhappiness will be the result, if it be forced in any way by any being. Therefore, according to Vedanta human affection and Divine Love each has its value in its own sphere.

### Songs of Kabir

He who is meek and contented, he who has an equal vision, whose mind is filled with the fullness of acceptance and of rest;
He who has seen Him and touched Him, he is freed from all fear and trouble.
To him the perpetual thought of God is like sandal paste smeared on the body, to him nothing else is delight:
His work and his rest are filled with music: he sheds abroad the radiance of love.
Kabir says: "Touch His feet, who is one and indivisible, immutable and peaceful; who fills all vessels to the brim with joy, and whose form is love."

I laugh when I hear that the fish in the water is thirsty:
You do not see that the Real is in your home, and you wander from forest to forest listlessly!
Here is the truth! Go where you will, to Benares or to Mathura; if you do not find your soul, the world is unreal to you.

He is dear to me indeed who can call back the wanderer to his home. In the home is the true union, in the home is enjoyment of life: why should I forsake my home and wander in the forest? If Brahma helps me to realize truth, verily I will find both bondage and deliverance in home.

He is dear to me indeed who has power to dive deep into Brahma; whose mind loses itself with ease in His contemplation.

He is dear to me who knows Brahma, and can dwell on His supreme truth in meditation; and who can play the melody of the Infinite by uniting love and renunciation in life.

Kabir says: "The home is the abiding place; in the home is reality; the home helps to attain Him Who is real. So stay where you are, and all things shall come to you in time."

To what shore would you cross, O my heart? there is no traveller before you, there is no road:

Where is the movement, where is the rest, on that shore?

There is no water; no boat, no boatman is there;

There is not so much as a rope to tow the boat, nor a man to draw it.

No earth, no sky, no time, no thing, is there; no shore, no ford!

There, there, is neither body nor mind: and where is the place that shall still the thirst of the soul? You shall find naught in that emptiness.

Be strong, and enter into your own body: for there your foothold is firm. Consider it well, O my heart! go not elsewhere.

Kabir says: "Put all imaginations away, and stand fast in that which you are."

BETWEEN the poles of the conscious and the unconscious, there has the mind made a swing:
Thereon hang all beings and all worlds, and that swing never ceases its sway.
Millions of beings are there: the sun and the moon in their courses are there:
Millions of ages pass, and the swing goes on.
All swing! the sky and the earth and the air and the water; and the Lord Himself taking form:
And the sight of this has made Kabir a servant.

THE moon shines in my body, but my blind eyes cannot see it:
The moon is within me, and so is the sun.
The unstruck drum of Eternity is sounded within me; but my deaf ears cannot hear it.

So long as man clamours for the "I" and the "Mine," his works are as naught:
When all love of the "I" and the "Mine" is dead, then the work of the Lord is done.
For work has no other aim than the getting of knowledge;
When that comes, then work is put away.

The flower blooms for the fruit; when the fruit comes, the flower withers.
The musk is in the deer, but it seeks it not within itself: it wanders in quest of grass.

# SELECTIONS FROM GITANJALI
## SONG OFFERINGS
### Rabindranath Tagore

Life of my life, I shall ever try to keep my body pure, knowing that thy living touch is upon all my limbs.

I shall ever try to keep all untruths out from my thoughts, knowing that thou art that truth which has kindled the light of reason in my mind.

I shall ever try to drive all evils away from my heart and keep my love in flower, knowing that thou hast thy seat in the inmost shrine of my heart.

And it shall be my endeavour to reveal thee in my actions, knowing it is thy power gives me strength to act.

I ask for a moment's indulgence to sit by thy side. The works that I have in hand I will finish afterwards.

Away from the sight of thy face my heart knows no rest nor respite, and my work becomes an endless toil in a shoreless sea of toil.

To-day the summer has come at my window with its sighs and murmurs and the bees are plying their minstrelsy at the court of the flowering grove.

Now it is time to sit quiet, face to face with thee, and to sing dedication of life in this silent and overflowing leisure.

LEAVE this chanting and singing and telling of beads! Whom dost thou worship in this lonely dark corner of a temple with doors all shut? Open thine eyes and see thy God is not before thee!

He is there where the tiller is tilling the hard ground and where the path-maker is breaking stones. He is with them in sun and in shower, and his garment is covered with dust. Put off thy holy mantle and even like him come down on the dusty soil!

Deliverance? Where is this deliverance to be found? Our master himself has joyfully taken upon him the bonds of creation; he is bound with us all for ever.

Come out of thy meditations and leave aside thy flowers and incense. What harm is there if thy clothes become tattered and stained? Meet him and stand by him in toil and in sweat of thy brow.

ON the day when the lotus bloomed, alas, my mind was straying, and I knew it not. My basket was empty and the flower remained unheeded.

Only now and again a sadness fell upon me, and

I started up from my dream and felt a sweet trace of a strange fragrance in the south wind.

That vague sweetness made my heart ache with longing and it seemed to me that it was the eager breath of the summer seeking for its completion.

I knew not then that it was so near, that it was mine, and that this perfect sweetness had blossomed in the depths of my own heart.

I CAME out alone on my way to my tryst. But who is this that follows me in the silent dark?

I move aside to avoid his presence but I escape him not.

He makes the dust rise from the earth with his swagger, he adds his loud voice to every word that I utter.

He is my own little self, my lord, he knows no shame; but I am ashamed to come to thy door in his company.

"PRISONER, tell me, who was it that bound you?"

"It was my master," said the prisoner. "I thought I could outdo everybody in the world in wealth and power, and I amassed in my treasure-house the money due to my king. When sleep overcame me I lay upon the bed that was for my lord, and on waking up I found I was a prisoner in my own treasure-house."

"Prisoner, tell me, who was it that wrought this unbreakable chain?"

"It was I," said the prisoner, "who forged this chain very carefully. I thought my invincible power would hold the world captive leaving me in a freedom undisturbed. Thus night and day I worked at the chain with huge fires and cruel hard strokes. When at last the work was done and the links were complete and unbreakable, I found that it held me in its grip."

THIS is my prayer to thee, my lord — strike, strike at the root of penury in my heart.

Give me the strength lightly to bear my joys and sorrows.

Give me the strength to make my love fruitful in service.

Give me the strength never to disown the poor or bend my knees before insolent might.

Give me the strength to raise my mind high above daily trifles.

And give me the strength to surrender my strength to thy will with love.

I THOUGHT that my voyage had come to its end at the last limit of my power, — that the path before me was closed, that provisions were exhausted and the time come to take shelter in a silent obscurity.

But I find that thy will knows no end in me. And when old words die out on the tongue, new melodies break forth from the heart; and where the old tracks are lost, new country is revealed with its wonders.

ON the seashore of endless worlds children meet. The infinite sky is motionless overhead and the restless water is boisterous. On the seashore of endless worlds the children meet with shouts and dances.

They build their houses with sand and they play with empty shells. With withered leaves they weave their boats and smilingly float them on the vast deep. Children have their play on the seashore of worlds.

They know not how to swim, they know not how to cast nets. Pearl fishers dive for pearls, merchants sail in their ships, while children gather pebbles and scatter them again. They seek not for hidden treasures, they know not how to cast nets.

The sea surges up with laughter and pale gleams the smile of the sea beach. Death-dealing waves sing meaningless ballads to the children, even like a mother while rocking her baby's cradle. The sea plays with children, and pale gleams the smile of the sea beach.

On the seashore of endless worlds children meet. Tempest roams in the pathless sky, ships get wrecked in the trackless water, death is abroad and children play. On the seashore of endless worlds is the great meeting of children.

THE sleep that flits on baby's eyes — does anybody know from where it comes? Yes, there is a rumour that it has its dwelling where, in the fairy village among shadows of the forest dimly lit with glowworms, there hang two timid buds of enchantment. From there it comes to kiss baby's eyes.

The smile that flickers on baby's lips when he sleeps — does anybody know where it was born? Yes, there is a rumour that a young pale beam of a crescent moon touched the edge of a vanishing autumn cloud, and there the smile was first born in the dream of a dew-washed morning — the smile that flickers on baby's lips when he sleeps.

The sweet, soft freshness that blooms on baby's limbs — does anybody know where it was hidden so long? Yes, when the mother was a young girl it lay pervading her heart in tender and silent mystery of love — the sweet, soft freshness that has bloomed on baby's limbs.

WHEN I bring to you coloured toys, my child, I understand why there is such a play of colours on clouds, on water, and why flowers are painted in tints — when I give coloured toys to you, my child.

When I sing to make you dance I truly know why there is music in leaves, and why waves send their chorus of voices to the heart of the listening earth — when I sing to make you dance.

When I bring sweet things to your greedy hands I know why there is honey in the cup of the flower and why fruits are secretly filled with sweet juice — when I bring sweet things to your greedy hands.

When I kiss your face to make you smile, my darling, I surely understand what the pleasure is that streams from the sky in morning light, and what delight that is which the summer breeze brings to my body — when I kiss you to make you smile.

WHEN the creation was new and all the stars shone in their first splendour, the gods held their assembly in the sky and sang "O the picture of perfection! the joy unalloyed!"

But one cried of a sudden — "It seems that somewhere there is a break in the chain of light and one of the stars has been lost."

The golden string of their harp snapped, their song stopped, and they cried in dismay — "Yes, that lost star was the best, she was the glory of all heavens!"

From that day the search is unceasing for her, and the cry goes on from one to the other that in her the world has lost its one joy!

Only in the deepest silence of night the stars smile and whisper among themselves — "Vain is this seeking! Unbroken perfection is over all."

ON many an idle day have I grieved over lost time. But it is never lost, my lord. Thou hast taken every moment of my life in thine own hands.

Hidden in the heart of things thou art nourishing seeds into sprouts, buds into blossoms, and ripening flowers into fruitfulness.

I was tired and sleeping on my idle bed and imagining all work had ceased. In the morning I woke up and found my garden full with wonders of flowers.

Ever in my life have I sought thee with my songs. It was they who led me from door to door, and with them have I felt about me, searching and touching my world.

It was my songs that taught me all the lessons I ever learnt; they showed me secret paths, they brought before my sight many a star on the horizon of my heart.

They guided me all the day long to the mysteries of the country of pleasure and pain, and, at last, to what palace gate have they brought me in the evening at the end of my journey?

# THE SAYINGS OF RAMAKRISHNA
## Attaining Perfection

THERE are two classes of people who attain perfection in this world: those who get the truth and become silent, enjoying it all to themselves without any thought of others; people of the other class get the truth and cannot find pleasure in keeping it to themselves, but cry out in a trumpet voice to all, "Come ye and enjoy the truth with us."

THIS world is like a stage where men perform many parts under various disguises. They do not like to take off the mask, unless they have played for some time. Let them play for a while, and then they will leave off the mask of their own accord.

THOSE who seek for fame are under delusion. They forget that everything is ordained by the Great Disposer of all things, — the Supreme Being, and that all is due to the Lord and to no one else. It is the wise who say always, "It is Thou, It is Thou, O Lord," but the ignorant and the deluded say, "It is I, It is I."

THE following are among those who cannot gain self-knowledge. Those who boast of learning, those who are proud of knowledge, and those who are vain of riches. If one says to these, "In such and such a place there is a good Sannyâsin, will you come to see him?" they will invariably make some excuses and say that they cannot go; but in their minds they think they are men of high positions, why should they go to another?

## Money and Riches

There is nothing to be proud of in money. If you say that you are rich, there are richer and richer men than you, in comparison with whom you are a mere beggar. After dusk when the glow-worms make their appearance, they think, "We are giving light to the world." But when the stars rise, their pride is gone. Then the stars begin to think, "We are shedding light on the universe." After some time the moon ascends the sky, and the stars are humiliated and look melancholy. So again the moon begins to be proud and think that by her light the world is lighted, and smiles and bathes in beauty and cheerfulness. But lo! the dawn proclaims the advent of the rising sun on the eastern horizon. Where is the moon now? If they who think themselves rich ponder over these natural facts, they will never, never boast of their riches again.

## God

You see many stars at night in the sky but find them not when the sun rises; can you say that there are no stars in the heaven of day? So, O man! because you behold not God in the days of your ignorance, say not that there is no God.

MANY are the names of God and infinite the forms that lead us to know Him. In whatsoever name or form you desire to call Him, in that very form and name you will see Him.

As one can ascend to the top of a house by means of a ladder or a bamboo or a staircase or a rope, so divers are the ways and means to approach God, and every religion in the world shows one of these ways.

HE who tries to give an idea of God by mere book learning, is like the man who tries to give an idea of Kasi (Benares) by means of a map or picture.

GOD is in all men but all men are not in God: that is the reason why they suffer.

THE magnetic needle always points towards the North, and hence it is that the sailing vessel does not lose her course. So long as the heart of man is directed towards God, he cannot be lost in the ocean of worldliness.

### Spiritual Life

EVERY man should follow his own religion. A Christian should follow Christianity, a Mahomedan should follow Mahomedanism, and so on. For the Hindus the ancient path, the path of the Aryan *Rishis*, is the best.

PEOPLE partition off their lands by means of boundaries, but no one can partition off the all-embracing sky overhead. The indivisible sky surrounds all and includes all. So common man in ignorance says, "My religion is the only one, my religion is the best." But when his heart is illumined by true knowledge, he knows that above all these wars of sects and sectarians presides the one indivisible, eternal, all-knowing Bliss.

THE pearl oyster that contains the precious pearl is in itself of very little value, but it is essential for the growth of the pearl. The shell itself may prove to be of no use to the man who has got the pearl. So ceremonies and rites may not be necessary for him who has attained the Highest Truth — God.

MAN is born in this world with two tendencies — the Vidyâ tendency, or tendency towards liberation, and the Avidyâ tendency, or tendency towards world and bondage. When born, both tendencies are in equilibrium like the scales of a balance. The world soon places its enjoyments and pleasures in one scale, and the spirit its attractions on the other; and if the intellect chooses the world, the worldly scale becomes heavy and gravitates towards the earth. But if it chooses the spirit, the spiritual scale gravitates towards God.

THE soul reincarnates in a body of which it was thinking just before its last departure from this world. Devotional practices may therefore be seen to be very necessary. When by constant practice no worldly ideas arise in the mind, then the God-idea alone fills the soul and does not leave it even when on the brink of eternity.

## EGOISM

EGOISM is like a cloud that keeps God hidden from our sight. If by the mercy of the Guru egoism vanishes, God is seen in His full glory.

IF one acquires the conviction that everything is done by God's will, that one is only the tool in the hands of God, then is one free even in this life. "Thou doest Thy work, they say, 'I do it!'"

PONDER deep and thou shalt know that there is no such thing as "I." As by continually peeling off the skin of an onion, so on analyzing the ego it will be found that there is not any real entity corresponding to the ego. The ultimate result of all such analysis is God. When egoism drops away Divinity manifests itself.

IF one ponders over the "I," and tries to find out what it is, one sees it is only a word which denotes egoism. It is extremely difficult to shake off. Then one says, "You wicked 'I,' if you will not go by any means, remain as the servant of God." This is called the "ripe I."

IF you feel proud, feel so in the thought that you are the servant of God.

### ON LOVE

THERE are three kinds of love, — unselfish (Samârthâ), mutual (Sâman jasâ), and selfish (Sadhârni). The unselfish love is of the highest kind. The lover only minds the welfare of the beloved and does not care for his own sufferings. In mutual love the lover not only wants the happiness of his beloved but has an eye towards his own happiness also. It is middling. The selfish love is the lowest. It only looks towards its own happiness, no matter whether the beloved suffers weal or woe.

*Q.* WHY does the God-lover renounce everything for Him?
*A.* The moth, after seeing the light, never returns to darkness; the ant dies in the sugar-heap, but never retreats therefrom; similarly the God-lover gladly sacrifices his life for the attainment of Divine bliss and cares for nothing else.

## On Meditation

IF you have a mind to live unattached from the world, you should first practise devotion in solitude for some time, — say a year, or six months, or a month, or at least twelve days. During the period of retirement you should meditate constantly upon God and pray to Him for Divine Love. You should revolve in your mind the thought that there is nothing in the world that you may call your own; those whom you think your own will pass away in no time. God is really your own, He is your All-in-All. How to obtain Him should be your only concern.

KEEP thyself aloof at the time of thy devotions from those who scoff at them and from those who ridicule piety and the pious.

KEEP thine own sentiments and faith to thyself. Do not talk about them abroad. Otherwise thou wilt be a great loser.

## The Truly Religious

THE truly religious man is he who does not commit any sin even when he is alone, because God sees him, though no man may see him. He who can resist the temptation of lust and gold in a lonely place unobserved by any man, through the fear that God sees him, and who through such fear does not even think an evil thought, is truly a religious man. But he who practises religion for the sake of show and through the fear of public opinion has no religion in him.

THAT man, who living in the midst of the temptations of the world attains perfection, is the true hero.

THOSE who live in the world and try to find salvation are like soldiers that fight protected by the breastwork of a fort, while the ascetics who renounce the world in search of God are like soldiers fighting in the open field. To fight from within the fort is more convenient and safer than to fight in the open field.

### THE DIVINE MOTHER

*Q.* WHY does the God-lover find such ecstatic pleasure in addressing the Deity as Mother?

*A.* Because the child is more free with its mother, and consequently she is dearer to the child than any one else.

A LOGICIAN once asked Sri Râmakrishna, "What are knowledge, knower, and the object known?" To which he replied, "Good man, I do not know all these niceties of scholastic learning. I know only my Mother Divine, and that I am Her son."

PRAY to the Divine Mother in this wise: Give me, O Mother! love that knows no incontinence and faith adamantine that cannot be shaken.

Woman and wealth have drowned the whole world in sin. Woman is disarmed when you view her as the manifestation of the Divine Mother.

## Miscellaneous Sayings

"To him who is perfect in meditation salvation is very near," is an old saying. Do you know when a man becomes perfect in meditation? When, as soon as he sits down to meditate, he becomes surrounded with Divine atmosphere and his soul communes with God.

He who at the time of contemplation is entirely unconscious of everything outside — so much so that he would not know if birds were to make nests in his hair — has acquired the perfection of meditation.

So long as one does not become simple like a child one does not get Divine il umination. Forget all the worldly knowledge that thou hast acquired and become as ignorant as a child, and then wilt thou get the Divine wisdom.

To live in the world or to leave it depends upon the will of God. Therefore work, leaving everything to Him. What else can you do?

As dry leaves are blown about here and there by the wind and have no choice of their own and make no exertion; so those who depend upon

God move in harmony with His will, and can have no will and put forth no effort of their own.

THE vanities of all others may gradually die out, but the vanity of a saint as regards his sainthood is hard indeed to wear away.

BE as devoid of vanity as the castaway leaf before the high wind.

VANITY is like a heap of rubbish or ashes on which the water, as soon as it falls, dries away. Prayers and contemplations produce no effect on the heart puffed up with vanity.

THE scale that is heavy bends down, but the lighter scale of the balance rises up. So the man of merit and ability is always humble and meek, but the fool is always puffed up with vanity.

LUNATICS, drunkards and children sometimes give out the truth unconsciously, as if inspired by heaven.

MANY with a show of humility say, "I am like a low worm grovelling in the dust"; thus always thinking themselves worms, in time they become weak in spirit like worms. Let not despondency ever enter into thy heart; despair is the great enemy of progress in one's path. As a man thinketh, so he becometh.

THE mind attached to lust and wealth is like the unripe betel-nut attached to its shell; so long as the betel-nut is not ripe it remains fixed to its shell by its juice, but when the juicy substance dries by time, the nut becomes detached from its shell and is felt rolling inside the shell, if shaken. So when the juice of attachment to gold and lust is dried up, the man becomes free.

# ACKNOWLEDGMENT
# BIBLIOGRAPHY AND SOURCES

GRATEFUL acknowledgment is made to the following publishers and authors for their courtesy in permitting the printing in this book of copyrighted matter from the following sources:

*The Songs of Kabir.* Translated by RABINDRANATH TAGORE, The Macmillan Company, New York.

*Getanjale.* By RABINDRANATH TAGORE, The Macmillan Company New York.

*The Sayings of Ramakrishna.* Compiled by SWAMI ABHEDANANDA, The Vedanta Society, New York.

*Human Affection and Divine Love.* SWAMI ABHEDANANDA, Vedanta Society, New York.

*India and Her People.* By SWAMI ABHEDANANDA, Vedanta Society, New York.

*How to Be a Yoga.* SWAMI ABHEDANANDA, Vedanta Society, New York.

*The Path of Devotion.* SWAMI PARAMANANDA, Vedanta Centre, Boston, Mass.

*The Way of Peace.* SWAMI PARAMANANDA, Vedanta Centre, Boston, Mass.

*Rája Yoga.* SWAMI VIVEKANANDA, Brentano's, New York.

*Inspired Talks,* SWAMI VIVEKANANDA, Vedanta Society, New York.

*The Six Systems of Indian Philosophy.* MAX MULLER, Longmans Green & Co., New York.

*The Oxford History of India.* VINCENT A. SMITH, The Oxford University Press, New York.

*The Five Princes.* F. J. GOULD, J. M. Dent & Son, London.

## 274 BIBLIOGRAPHY AND SOURCES

*What Love Can Do.* F. J. GOULD, J. M. Dent & Son, London.
*The Vedic Hymns.* Translated by MAX MULLER, Oxford University Press, New York.
*Yoga Aphorisms of Patanjali.* Translated by WM. Q. JUDGE, Theosophical Society.
*The Song Celestial.* Translated by Sir EDWIN ARNOLD, Kegan Paul, Trench, Trübner & Co., London.
*Indian Poetry.* Translated by Sir EDWIN ARNOLD, Kegan Paul, Trench, Trübner & Co., London.
*The Upanishads.* Translated by MAX MULLER, Oxford University Press, New York.
*The Bhagavad Gita.* Translated by CHARLES JOHNSTON, Quarterly Book Co., New York.
*Patanjalis Yoga Aphorisms.* Translated by CHARLES JOHNSTON.
*Rabindranath Tagore; The Man and His Poetry.* By BASANTA KOOMER ROY, Dodd, Mead & Co., New York.
*History of Indian Literature.* By ALBRECHT WEBBER, Kegan Paul, Trench, Trübner & Co., London.
*The History of the Aryan Rule in India.* By E. B. HAVELL, Frederick A. Stokes Co., New York.
*India.* By PIERRE LOTI, Frederick A. Stokes Co., New York.
*India and Its Faiths.* By JAMES B. PRATT, PH.D., Houghton Mifflin Co., Boston, Mass.
*The System of Vedanta.* By PAUL DEUSSEN, Open Court Co., Chicago, Ill.
*The Philosophy of Ancient India.* By Prof. RICHARD GARBE, Open Court Co., Chicago, Ill.
*Classical Dictionary of Hindu Mythology and Religion.* By Prof. J. DAWSON, Kegan Paul, Trench, Trübner & Co. London.
*The Sacred Books of India.* Oxford University Press, New York.
*The Religion of the Sikhs.* By DOROTHY FIELD, E. P. Dutton & Co., New York.

BIBLIOGRAPHY AND SOURCES 275

*The Heart of India.* By L. D. BARNETT, M.A., E. P. Dutton & Co., New York.

*Brahma-Knowledge.* By L. D. BARNETT, M.A., E. P. Dutton & Co., New York.

*The Ramayana and Maha-Bharata.* Translated by ROMESH DUTT, E. P. Dutton & Co., New York.

*The Gospel of Ramakrishna.* Translated by SWAMI ABHEDANANDA, Vedanta Society, New York.

# GLOSSARY

[*Reprinted from "Raja Yoga," by Swami Vivekananda. Brentano's, Publishers, New York.*]

### A FEW SIMPLE HELPS TO PRONUNCIATION

á like *a* in far;  
a almost like *u* in but;  
e like *a* in name;  
í like *ee* in see;  

ú like *oo* in too;  
s like *sh* in ship;  
ch like *ch* in rich;  
ai like *i* in fine.

No attempt is made to give the finer distinctions of Sanskrit pronunciation, as a thorough knowledge of the language would be needed to grasp them.

In this glossary are to be found words commonly used in books and pamphlets on Vedânta, as well as those that are employed in this volume.

*Abhaya.* Fearlessness.
*Abhâva.* Bereft of quality.
*Abheda.* Non-separateness; sameness; without distinction.
*Abhidhyâ.* Not coveting others' goods, not thinking vain thoughts, not brooding over injuries received from others.
*Abhighâta.* Impediment.
*Abhimâna.* Pride.
*Abhinivêsa.* Attachment to life.
*Abhyâsa.* Practice.
*Âchârya.* Great spiritual teacher.
*Âdarsa.* A mirror — a term sometimes used to denote the finer power of vision developed by the *Yogî.*
*Âdhidaivika.* Supernatural.
*Adhikâri.* One qualified as a seeker of wisdom.
*Aditi.* The infinite, the goddess of the sky.
*Âditya.* The Sun.
*Âdityas.* Twelve planetary spirits.
*Adharma.* Absence of virtue; unrighteousness.
*Adrogha.* Not injuring.
*Adrogha-Vâk.* One who does not harm others even by words.

# GLOSSARY

*Advaita.* (A-dvaita) Non-dualism. The monistic system of *Vedánta* philosophy.
*Advaitin.* A follower of *Advaita.*
*Adhyása.* Reflection, as the crystal reflects the color of the object before it. Superimposition of qualities of one object over another, as of the snake on the rope.
*Agni.* The god of fire. Later, the Supreme God of the Vedas.
*Aham.* "I."
*Aham-Brahmásmi.* "I am Brahman."
*Ahamkára.* Egoism. Self-consciousness.
*Áhára.* Gathering in, — as food to support the body or the mind.
*Ahimsá.* Non-injuring in thought, word, or deed.
*Ahimsaka.* One who practises *Ahimsá.*
*Ájná.* The sixth lotos of the *Yogis,* corresponding to a nerve centre in the brain, behind the eyebrows. Divine perception.
*Ajnáta.* One who has attained divine wisdom.
*Ákása.* The all-pervading material of the universe.
*Akbar.* Mogul Emperor of India, 1542–1605.
*Akhanda.* Undivided.
*Akhanda Satchidánanda.* "The undivided Existence — Knowledge — Bliss Absolute."
*Álambana.* Objective contemplation. The things which are supports to the mind in its travel Godwards.
*Amritatvam.* Immortality.
*Anáhata.* lit. "unstruck sound." The fourth lotos of the *Yogis* in the *ushumná,* opposite the heart.
*Ánanda.* Bliss.
*Ananya-Bhakti.* Worship of one particular Deity in preference to all others. In a higher sense, it is seeing all Deities as but so many forms of the One God. Singleness of love and worship.
*Anavasáda.* Cheerfulness, not becoming dejected. Strength, both mental and physical.
*Animá.* Attenuation.
*Antahkarana.* Internal organ. The mind with its three functions, the cogitative faculty, the determinative faculty and the egoism.
*Antaryámin.* The name of *Ísvara,* — meaning, He who knows everything that is going on within (*antara*) every mind.
*Antarárána.* The *Yogi* who rests in the final contemplation of the Supreme Lord (*Ísvara*).
*Anubhava.* Realization.
*Anuddharsa.* Absence of excessive merriment.
*Anumána.* Inference.
*Anurakti.* The attachment that comes after the knowledge of the nature of God.

# GLOSSARY

*Anurāga.* Great attachment to *Iśvara.*
*Anuvāda.* A statement referring to something already known.
*Apakshiyate.* To decay.
*Apāna.* One of the five manifestations of *prāna.* The nerve current in the body which governs the organs of excretion.
*Aparapratyaksha.* Super-sensuous perception.
*Aparāvidyā.* Lower knowledge; knowledge of externals.
*Aparigraha.* Non-receiving of gifts; not indulging in luxuries.
*Apas.* One of the elements; water; liquid.
*Aprātikūlya.* State of sublime resignation.
*Āpta.* One who has attained to realization of God; one who is self-illumined.
*Āptavākyam.* Words of an *Āpta.*
*Apura.* Merit.
*Āranyakas.* The ancient *Rishis,* dwellers in the forest, also a name given to the books composed by them.
*Aristha.* Portents or signs by which a *Yogī* can foretell the exact time of his death.
*Ārjavam.* Straightforwardness.
*Arjuna.* The hero of the *Bhagavad Gītā,* to whom Krishna (in the form of a charioteer) taught the great truths of the *Vedānta* philosophy.
*Artha.* Meaning.
*Arthavattva.* Fruition.
*Arūpa.* (A-rūpa) Without form.
*Āryāvarta.* The land of the Aryans. The name applied by the Hindus to Northern India.
*Asamprajnāta.* The highest super-conscious state.
*Āsana.* Position of the body during meditation.
*Asat.* Non-being or existence. Opposite of *Sat.* Applied to the changing existence of the universe.
*Asmitā.* Non-discrimination.
*Aśoka.* A noted Buddhist King, 259-222 B.C.
*Āśrama.* Hermitage.
*Āsvāda.* lit. "taste,"— applied to the finer faculty of taste developed by the *Yogī.*
*Asteyam.* Non-stealing.
*Asti.* To be, or exist.
*Atharva Veda.* That portion of the *Veda* which treats of psychic powers.
*Athāto Brahma-jijnāsā.* "Then therefore, the enquiry into *Brahman.*" [*Vedānta Sutra,* 1-1-I.]
*Atikrānta-Bhavaniya.* The stage of meditation which ends with what is called "Cloud (or Showerer) of Virtue" *Samādhi.*
*Atithi.* A guest.
*Ātman.* The Eternal Self.

*Âvarana.* Coverings (of the mind).
*Avatâra.* A divine Incarnation.
*Avidyâ.* Ignorance.
*Âvritti-rasakrit-upadeśât.* "Repetition (of the mental functions of knowing, meditating, etc., is required) on account of the text giving instructions more than once." [*Vedânta Sutra*, 1-1-IV.]
*Avyaktam.* Indiscrete; undifferentiated. Stage of nature, when there is no manifestation.

*Bâhya-Bhakti.* External devotion (as worship through rites, symbols, ceremonials, etc., of God).
*Bandha.* Bondage.
*Banyan-Tree.* (*Ficus Indica*) Indian fig tree; the branches drop roots to the ground, which grow and form new trunks.
*Bhagavad-Gîtâ.* "The Holy Song." A gem of Indian literature containing the essence of the *Vedânta* philosophy.
*Bhagavân.* lit. "Possessor of all powers." A title meaning Great Lord.
*Bhagavân-Râmakrishna.* A great Hindu prophet and teacher of the nineteenth century, 1835-1886. [See "Life and Sayings of Śrî Râmakrishna" by F. Max Müller. London, 1898. Longmans, Green & Co., and Charles Scribner's Sons. New York.]
*Bhâgavata-Purâna.* One of the principal *Purânas*.
*Bhakta.* A great lover of God.
*Bhakti.* Intense love for God.
*Bhakti-Yoga.* Union with the Divine through devotion.
*Bharata.* A great *Yogî* who suffered much from his excessive attachment to a deer which he brought up as a pet.
*Bhâshya.* A commentary.
*Bhautika.* Pertaining to the *Bhûtas*, or elements.
*Bhâvanâ.* Pondering; meditation.
*Bheda.* Separateness.
*Bhikshu.* A religious mendicant, a term now usually applied to the Buddhist monks.
*Bhoga.* Enjoyment of sense objects.
*Bhoja.* The annotator of the Yoga Aphorisms.
*Bhûtas.* Gross elements.
*Bodha.* Intelligence.
*Brahmâ.* The Creator of the universe.
*Brahmacharya.* Chastity in thought, word and deed.
*Brahmachârin.* One who has devoted himself to continence and the pursuit of spiritual wisdom.
*Brahmaloka.* The world of *Brahmâ*, the highest heaven.
*Brahman.* The One Existence, the Absolute.
*Brâhmana.* A "twice-born man," a Brahmin.

*Brâhmanas.* Those portions of the Vedas which state the rules for the employment of the hymns at the various ceremonials. Each of the four *Vedas* has its own *Brâhmana.*

*Brahma-Sutra-Bôdshya.* Commentary on the aphorisms of *Vedânta.*

*Brahmavâddin.* Teacher of *Brahman,* one who speaks or teaches of Brahman or Absolute Being.

*Brahmavidyâ.* Knowledge of *Brahman,* the supreme wisdom that leads to *Mukti.*

*Brahmayoga.* The *Yoga* which leads to the realization of the *Brahman* (Chap. VIII of the *Bhagavad Gîtâ* is called by that name).

*Brahmin.* An Anglicized form of *Brâhmana,* a member of the *Brâhmana* caste.

*Buddha.* lit. "the Enlightened," the name given to one of the greatest Incarnations recognized by the Hindus, born sixth century B.C.

*Buddhi.* The determinative faculty.

*Chaitanya.* Pure intelligence. Name of a great Hindu sage (born 1485) who is regarded as a Divine Incarnation.

*Chândogya Upanishad.* One of the oldest *Upanishads* of the *Sâma-Veda.*

*Chârvâka.* A materialist.

*Chidâkâśâ.* The space of knowledge, where the Soul shines in its own nature.

*Chitta.* "Mind-stuff." (The fine material out of which the mind has been manufactured.)

*Chittâkâśâ.* The mental space.

*Dakshinâ.* Offering made to a priest, or teacher, at religious ceremonies.

*Dama.* Control of the organs.

*Dâna.* Charity.

*Dâsya.* "Servantship"; the state of being a devoted servant of God.

*Dayâ.* Mercy, compassion, doing good to others without hope of return.

*Deha.* Matter, gross body.

*Devadatta.* "God-given."

*Devas.* The "shining ones," semi-divine beings representing states attained by workers of good.

*Devaloka.* Abode of the gods.

*Devayâna.* The path which leads to the sphere of the gods, or the different heavens.

*Devî-Bhâgavata.* One of the *Purânas,* which describes the deeds of the Divine Mother.

*Dhârânâ.* Holding the mind to one thought for twelve seconds. Concentration.

*Dharma.* Virtue. Religious duty.
*Dharma-megha.* "Cloud of virtue" (applied to a kind of *Samâdhi*).
*Dhyâna.* Meditation.
*Dhyânamârga.* The way to knowledge through meditation.
*Dwandas.* Dualities in nature, as heat and cold, pleasure and pain, etc., etc.
*Dvesha.* Aversion.
*Dyâva-Prithivî.* Heaven (and) Earth.

*Ekâgra.* Concentrated state of the mind.
*Ekam.* One.
*Eka-Nisthâ.* Intense devotion to one chosen ideal.
*Ekânta-Bhakti.* Singleness of love and devotion to God.
*Ekâtma-Vâdam.* Monism. The theory, according to which there is only one intelligent Entity. Pure idealism.
*Ekâyana.* The one stay or support of all things, — hence the Lord.

*Ganapati.* One of the Hindu deities.
*Ganeśa.* A woman sage mentioned in the *Upanishads.* She practised *Yoga* and attained to the highest super-conscious state.
*Gârgi.* God of wisdom and "remover of obstacles." He is always invoked at the commencement of every important undertaking.
*Gauni.* Preparatory stage of *Bhakti-Yoga.*
*Gâyatri.* A certain most holy verse of the *Vedas.*
*Ghata.* A jar.
*Gopis.* Shepherdesses, worshippers of *Krishna.*
*Grahana.* Sense-perception.
*Grihastha.* A householder, head of a family.
*Gunas.* Qualities, attributes.
*Guru.* lit. "the dispeller of darkness." A religious teacher who removes the ignorance of the pupil. The real *guru* is a transmitter of the spiritual impulse that quickens the spirit and awakens a genuine thirst for religion.

*Hamsa.* The *Jîva,* or individual soul.
*Hanumân.* The great *Bhakta* hero of the *Râmâyana.*
*Hari.* lit. "One who steals the hearts and reason of all by His beauty," hence the Lord, a name of God.
*Hatha Yoga.* The science of controlling body and mind, but with no spiritual end in view, bodily perfection being the only aim.
*Hatha-Yogî* (or *Yogin*). One who practices "*Hatha-Yoga.*"
*Hiranyagarbha.* lit. "golden wombed." Applied to *Brahmâ,* the Creator, as producing the universe out of Himself.
*Hum.* A mystic word used in meditation as symbolic of the highest Bliss.

## GLOSSARY

*Idâ.* The nerve current on the left side of the spinal cord; the left nostril.
*Indra.* Ruler of the gods.
*Indriyâni.* Sense organs.
*Indriyas.* The internal organs of perception.
*Isâna.* One of the *devas*.
*Ishtam.* Chosen ideal (from "*ish*," to wish). That aspect of God which appeals to one most.
*Ishta Nisthâ.* Devotion to one ideal.
*Ishtâpûrta.* The works which bring as reward the enjoyments of the heavens.
*Isvara.* The Supreme Ruler; the highest possible conception through reason, of the Absolute, which is beyond all thought.
*Îsvarapranidhâna.* Meditation on *Isvara*.
*Isvara Pranidhânâdvâ.* A *Sûtra* of *Patanjali* — entitled "By worship of the Supreme Lord."

*Jada.* Inanimate.
*Jâgrat.* Waking state.
*Jâti.* Species.
*Jâyate.* To be born.
*Jîva.* The individual soul. The one Self as appearing to be separated into different entities; corresponding to the ordinary use of the word "*soul.*"
*Jîvatman.* The *Âtman* manifesting as the *Jîva*.
*Jîvan Mukta.* lit. "Living Freedom." One who has attained liberation (*Mukti*) even while in the body.
*Jnâna.* Pure intelligence. Knowledge.
*Jnâna-chaksu.* One whose vision has been purified by the realization of the Divine.
*Jnânakânda.* The knowledge portion or philosophy of the *Vedas*.
*Jnâna-yajna.* "Wisdom-Sacrifice." Perfect unselfishness, purity and goodness, which lead to *Jnâna*, or supreme wisdom (*Moksha*).
*Jnâni* [or *Jnânin*]. One who seeks liberation through pure reason or philosophy.

*Kaivalya.* Isolation. Oneness with Absolute Being.
*Kâla.* Time.
*Kalpa.* A cycle (in evolution).
*Kalyâna.* Blessings.
*Kâma.* Desire.
*Kapila.* Author of the *Sânkhya* philosophy, and the father of the Hindu Evolutionists.
*Kapilavastu.* Birthplace of *Gautama* the *Buddha*.

# GLOSSARY

*Káriká.* A running commentary.
*Karma.* Work or action, also effects of actions; the law of cause and effect in the moral world.
*Karmakánda.* The ritualistic portion of the *Vedas.*
*Karmendriyas.* Organs of action.
*Karma-Yoga.* Union with the Divine through the unselfish performance of duty.
*Khanda.* Differentiated, or divided; division.
*Klesa.* Troubles.
*Krishna.* An Incarnation of God who appeared in India about 1400 B.C. Most of his teachings are embodied in the *Bhagavad-Gítá.*
*Kriyá.* Action, ritual, ceremonial.
*Kriyamána.* The *Karma* we are making at present.
*Kriyá-Yoga.* Preliminary *Yoga,* the performance of such acts as lead the mind higher and higher.
*Kshana.* Moments.
*Kshatriya.* Member of the warrior (or second) caste of ancient India.
*Kshetra.* lit. "the perishable," also "a field." Applied to the human body (as the field of action).
*Kshetrajna.* The knower of *Kshetra.* (*Gítá,* Chap. XII.) The soul.
*Kumbhaka.* Retention of the breath in the practice of *pránáyáma.*
*Kundalini.* lit. "the coiled-up." The residual energy, located according to the *Yogís,* at the base of the spine, and which in ordinary men produces dreams, imagination, psychical perceptions, etc., and which, when fully aroused and purified, leads to the direct perception of God.
*Kuntí.* The mother of the five *Pándavas,* the heroes who opposed the *Kauravas,* at the battle of *Kurukshetra,* the account of which forms the principal theme of the *Mahábhárata,* the Indian epic.
*Kurma.* The name of a nerve upon which the *Yogís* meditate.
*Kurma-Puráná.* One of the eighteen principal *Puránas.*
*Kuśa.* A kind of Indian grass used in religious rites.

*Madhubhumiha.* The second stage of the *Yogí* when he gets beyond the argumentative condition.
*Madhumati.* lit. "honeyed." The state when knowledge gives satisfaction as honey does.
*Mathurá.* Sweet. That form of *Bhakti* in which the relation of the devotee towards God is like that of a loving wife to her husband.
*Madvácbárya.* Commentator of the dualistic school of the *Vedánta* philosophy.
*Mahákáśa.* lit. "Great space" (applied to ordinary space).
*Mahápurusha.* Great Soul. (Incarnation.)
*Mahat.* lit. "The great one." Cosmic intelligence.

*Mahattattva.* Great principle. The ocean of intelligence evolved first from indiscrete nature, according to *Sânkhya* philosophy.
*Mahâyoga.* Seeing the Self as one with God.
*Maitrîya.* lit. "Full of compassion." The name of a Hindu sage.
*Manas.* The deliberative faculty of the mind.
*Manipûra.* lit. "Filled with jewels." The third lotos of the *Yogis*, opposite the navel (in the *Suṣumnâ*).
*Mantra.* Any prayer, holy verse, sacred or mystic word recited or contemplated during worship.
*Mantra-drashtâ.* "Seer of thought." One possessed of super-sensuous knowledge.
*Mâtrâs.* Seconds.
*Matha.* Monastery.
*Mathurâ* [Now known as "*Muttra*"]. Birthplace of *Krishna*.
*Mâyâ.* Mistaking the unreal and phenomenal for the real and eternal. Commonly translated illusion (lit. "which baffles all measurement").
*Mîmânsâ.* lit. "Solution of a problem." One of the six schools of Indian philosophy.
*Moksha.* Freedom, liberation (*Mukti*).
*Moksha-dharma.* The virtues which lead to liberation of the soul.
*Mrityu.* Death. Another name for *Yama*.
*Mukti.* Emancipation from rebirth.
*Mûlâdâra.* The basic lotos of the *Yogis*.
*Mumukshutvam.* Desire for liberation.
*Mundaka-Upanishad.* One of the twelve principal *Upanishads*.
*Muni.* A (religious) sage.

*Nâda.* Sound, finer than is heard by our ears.
*Nâda-Brahma.* The "*sound-Brahman*." The *Om*, that undifferentiated Word, which has produced all manifestation.
*Nâdi.* A tube along which something flows — as the blood currents, or nervous energies.
*Nâdi-suddhi.* lit. "purification of the channel through which the nerve currents flow." One of the elementary breathing exercises.
*Naishthika.* One possessed of a singleness of devotion towards a high ideal of life.
*Namah.* Salutation.
*Nâma-rûpa.* Name and form.
*Nâmaśakti.* The power of the name of God.
*Nârada.* The great "god-intoxicated" sage of ancient India, who is reputed to have possessed all the "powers" described in *Yoga* philosophy.
*Nârada-Sutra.* The Aphorisms of *Nârada* on *Bhakti*.

*Nárdyana.* "Mover on the waters," a title of *Vishnu.*
*Natarája.* lit. "Lord of the stage," sometimes used for God as the Lord of this vast stage, the universe.
*"Neti, Neti."* "Not this, not this."
*Nimitta.* Operative cause.
*Nirálambana.* lit. "supportless," a very high stage of meditation, according to *Yoga* philosophy.
*Nirbija.* lit. "Without seed." The highest form of *Samádhi* or superconscious state of the mind according to *Yoga* philosophy.
*Nirguna.* Without attributes or qualities.
*Nishkámakarma.* Unselfish action. To do good acts without caring for the results.
*Nitya.* Permanent, eternal.
*Nirukta.* Science dealing with etymology and the meaning of words.
*Nirvána.* Freedom; extinction or "blowing out" of delusions.
*Nirvichára.* Without discrimination.
*Nirvikalpa.* Changeless.
*Nirvitarka.* Without question or reasoning.
*Nivritti.* "Revolving away from."
*Nishthá.* Singleness of attachment.
*Niyama.* The virtues of cleanliness, contentment, mortification, study and self-surrender.
*Nyáya.* The school of Indian logic. The science of logical philosophy.

*Ojas.* lit. "The illuminating or bright." The highest form of energy attained by a constant practice of continence and purity.
*Om* or *Omkára.* The most holy word of the *Vedas.* A symbolic word meaning the Supreme Being, the Ocean of Knowledge and Bliss Absolute.
*Om tat sat.* lit. *"Om* That Existence." That Ocean of Knowledge and Bliss Absolute, the only Reality.

*Pada.* Foot.
*Páda.* Chapter.
*Pará.* Supreme.
*Pará-Bhakti.* Supreme devotion.
*Paramahamsa.* Supreme soul.
*Parávidyá.* Highest knowledge.
*Parinamate.* To ripen.
*Parjanya.* God of rain, and of the clouds.
*Patanjali.* Founder of the *Yoga* School of Philosophy.
*Pingalá.* The nerve-current on the right side of the spinal cord; also the right nostril.
*Pingalá.* A courtesan who abandoned her vicious life and became remarkable for her piety and virtue.

# GLOSSARY

*Pitris.* Forefathers, ancestors.
*Pradhâna.* lit. "The chief." The principal element; a name used for nature in *Sânkya* philosophy.
*Prajnâ.* Highest knowledge which leads to the realization of the Deity.
*Prajnâjyoti.* One who has been illumined with knowledge transcending the senses.
*Prakriti.* Nature.
*Prakritilayas.* Souls that have got all the powers that nature has by becoming one with nature.
*Prablâda.* The chief of *Bhaktas.* [Devotees.]
*Pramâna.* Means of proof.
*Pramêya.* Correct cognition.
*Prâna.* The sum total of the cosmic energy, the vital forces of the body.
*Prânâyâma.* Controlling the *prâna*.
*Pranidhâna.* Unceasing devotion.
*Prârabdha.* The works or *Karma* whose fruits we have begun to reap in this life.
*Prasankhyâna.* Abstract contemplation.
*Prathamakalpika.* Argumentative condition of the conscious *Yogî*.
*Pratibhâ.* Divine illumination.
*Pratîka.* lit. "Going towards." A finite symbol standing for the infinite *Brahman*.
*Pratimâ.* The use of images as symbols.
*Prativishaya.* That which is applied to the different objects, i. e., the organs of sense.
*Pratyâhâra.* Making the mind introspective.
*Pratyagâtman.* The internal self; the self-luminous.
*Pratyaksham.* Direct perception.
*Pravritti.* "Revolving towards."
*Prîti.* Pleasure in God.
*Prithivî.* One of the elements; earth; solids.
*Pûraka.* Inhalation.
*Purânas.* Writings containing the Hindu mythology.
*Puruśa.* The Soul.
*Pûrva-paksha.* The *prima facie* view.

*Q'uran.* The Mahommedan Scriptures.

*Râga.* Attachment to those things that please the senses.
*Râgânugâ.* The highest form of love and attachment to the Lord.
*Râja.* lit. "To shine." Royal.
*Râja Hamsa.* Swan.
*Rajas.* Activity. One of the three principles which form the essence of nature.

## GLOSSARY

*Rája Yoga.* lit. "Royal Yoga." The science of conquering the internal nature, for the purpose of realizing the Divinity within.
*Ráksbasa.* A demon.
*Rámánuja.* A noted commentator of the *Visbiśtadvaita* School of Philosophy (qualified monistic).
*Ráma.* An Incarnation of God, and hero of the celebrated epic — the *Rámáyana.*
*Rámáyana.* A celebrated Indian epic poem written by Valmiki, a sage.
*Rang.* A symbolic word for the highest wisdom.
*Rasáyanas.* The alchemists of ancient India.
*Recbaka.* Exhalation.
*Rig-Veda.* Oldest portion of the *Vedas*, composed of hymns.
*Risbi.* lit. "Seer of *mantras*" (thoughts). One possessed of supersensuous knowledge.
*Ritambbaráprajna.* One whose knowledge is truth-supporting.
*Rudra.* A name of a Vedic god.

*Śabda.* Sound.
*Śabdabrabma.* The creative word corresponding to the *Logos.*
*Śabda. Nisbtbam Jagat.* "Through sound the world stands."
*Sabija Yoga.* "Seeded" meditation (that is, where all seeds of future *Karma* are not yet destroyed).
*Saguna.* With qualities.
*Saguna-Brabma.* The qualified or lower Brahman.
*Saguna-vidyá.* Qualified knowledge.
*Sabaśrdra.* The "thousand-petalled lotos," a figurative expression of the *Yogís* describing the brain.
*Sakbya.* Friendship.
*Śakti.* Power.
*Sálokya.* Dwelling in the presence of God.
*Sama.* Not allowing the mind to externalize.
*Sáma-Veda.* The hymn portion of the *Veda*, or that portion which was sung during the ceremonies.
*Samádbi.* Super-consciousness.
*Samádbána.* Constant pratice.
*Samána.* The nerve current that controls the function of digestion.
*Sámányatadrisbta.* Inference based on superficial reasoning.
*Samápatti.* lit. "Treasures." Used in *Yoga* philosophy to indicate the different stages of meditation.
*Samarasa.* Equality.
*Samasti.* The universal.
*Sámipya.* Closeness to God.
*Samprajnáta.* The first stage of super-consciousness which comes through deep meditation.

# GLOSSARY

*Samsâra.* Endless cycle of manifestation.
*Samskâras.* Impressions in the mind-stuff that produces habits.
*Samyama.* lit. "Control." In the *Yoga* philosophy it is technically used for that perfect control of the powers of the mind, by which the *Yogî* can know anything in the universe.
*Sânandam.* The "blissful *Samâdhi.*" The third step of the *samprajnâta samâdhi*. The object of meditation in this state is the "thinking organ" bereft of activity and dullness. (*Rajas* and *Tamas.*)
*Sanchita.* The stored up, past *Karma*, whose fruits we are not reaping now, but which we shall have to reap in the future.
*Sândilya.* Writer of the Aphorisms of Divine Love (*Bhakti*) from the *Advaita* point of view.
*Sankarâchârya.* The great exponent and commentator of the non-dualistic school of Vedânta. He is supposed to have lived in India about the eighth century A.D.
*Sânkhya.* lit. "That which reveals truth perfectly." The name of a famous system of Indian philosophy, founded by the great sage Kapila.
*Sankocha.* Shrinking, contraction or non-manifestation.
*Sannyâsa.* Complete renunciation of all worldly position, property and name.
*Sannyâsin.* One who makes *Sannyâsa*, and lives a life of self-sacrifice, devoting himself entirely to religion.
*Sânta.* Peaceful or gentle love.
*Sânta-Bhakta.* A devotee who has attained to peace through the path of Divine love.
*Sântih.* Peace.
*Santosha.* Contentment.
*Sârupya.* Growing like God.
*Sâstra.* Books accepted as Divine authority. Sacred Scriptures.
*Sat.* Existence-Absolute.
*Satchidânanda.* "Existence — Knowledge — Bliss Absolute."
*Sattva.* Illumination material. One of the three principles which form the essence of nature.
*Sattva-pursbânyatâkhyâti.* The perception of the Self as different from the principles of nature.
*Sâttvika.* Having the *Sattva* quality highly developed, hence one who is pure and holy.
*Satyam.* Truthfulness.
*Saucham.* Cleanliness.
*Savichâra.* With discrimination. (A mode of meditation.)
*Savitarka.* Meditation with reasoning or question.
*Sâyujya.* Unity with Brahman.
*Sâkshi.* Witness.

## GLOSSARY

*Siddha-Guru.* A teacher who has attained *Mukti*.
*Siddhánta.* Decisive knowledge.
*Siddhas.* Semi-divine beings, or *Yogís*, who have attained supernatural powers.
*Siddhis.* The supernatural powers which come through the practice of *Yoga*.
*Sikshá.* The science dealing with pronunciation and accents.
*Sishya.* A student or disciple of a *Guru*.
*Siva.* The "Destroyer" of the Hindu trinity. Sometimes regarded in the Hindu mythology as the One God.
*Sivoham.* "*I am Śiva*" (or eternal bliss).
*Sloka.* Verse.
*Smriti.* (1) Memory. (2) Any authoritative religious book, except the *Vedas*.
*Soham.* "I am He."
*Soma.* A certain plant, the juice of which was used in the ancient sacrifices.
*Sphota.* The eternal, essential material of all ideas or names, which makes words possible, yet is not any definite word in a fully formed state. The inexpressible Manifestor behind all the expressed, sensible universe. The power through which the Lord creates the universe. Its symbol is the eternal *Om*.
*Sráddhá.* Strong faith in religion.
*Sravana.* (1) Hearing, the ears. (2) The finer power of hearing developed by the *Yogí*.
*Sri.* Holy or blessed.
*Sri Bhásbya.* Name of the qualified non-dualistic commentary of *Vedánta* by *Rámánuja*.
*Srotiyas.* lit. "High born," or born of a noble family. The Hindu students who know the *Vedas* by heart.
*Sruti.* The *Vedas*, so called because transmitted orally from father to son in ancient times. The *Vedas* are regarded by all orthodox Hindus as Divine revelation and as the supreme authority in religious matters.
*Sthiti.* Stability.
*Sthula Sarira.* Gross body.
*Sukshma Sarira* [sometimes called "*Linga Sarira*"]. Fine or subtle body.
*Sunya Váda.* Doctrine of the void; nihilism.
*Sushupti.* Deep, dreamless sleep.
*Sushumná.* The name given by the *Yogís* to the hollow canal which runs through the centre of the spinal cord.
*Sútra.* lit. "Thread." Usually means aphorism.
*Svádhisthána.* lit. "Abode of Self." Second lotos of the *Yogís*, between base of spine and the navel.

## GLOSSARY

*Svádhyáya.* Study.
*Sváhá!* "May it be perpetuated," or "So be it." An expression used in making oblation.
*Svapna.* The dream state.
*Svapnesvara.* Commentator of the Aphorisms of *Sándilya*.
*Svarúpa.* Natural form.
*Svasti.* A blessing, meaning "Good be unto you."
*Svátí.* Name of a star.
*Svarga.* Heaven.
*Svámi.* A title meaning "master," or "spiritual teacher."
*Svetasvatará-Upanishad.* One of the chief *Upanishads* of the *Yajur-Veda*.

*Tadiyatá.* lit. "His-ness." The state when a man has forgotten himself altogether, in his love for the Lord, and does not feel that anything belongs to him personally.
*Tamas.* "Darkness," inertia.
*Tanmátras.* Fine materials.
*Tantras.* Books held to be sacred by a certain sect in India.
*Tantríkas.* Followers of the *Tantras*.
*Tapas.* Controlling the body by fasting or other means. Austerity.
*Táraka.* Saviour.
*Tarka.* Question or reasoning.
*"Tat tvam asi."* "That thou art."
*Tattvas.* Categories, principles, truths.
*Tejas.* One of the elements; fire; heat.
*Titiksbá.* Ideal forbearance. "All-sufferingness."
*Trishná.* Thirst, desire.
*Tulsidás.* A great sage and poet who popularised the famous epic, the *Rámáyana*, by translating it from Sanskrit into Hindustani dialect.
*Turíya.* The fourth, or highest state of consciousness.
*Tyága.* Renunciation.

*Udána.* Nerve current governing the organs of speech, etc.
*Uddhársa.* Excessive merriment.
*Udgítba.* lit. "That which is chanted aloud," hence the *Pranava* or *Om*.
*Udgátba.* Awakening the *Kundalini*.
*Upádána.* The material cause of the world.
*Upádhi.* Limiting adjunct.
*Uparati.* Not thinking of things of the senses; discontinuing external religious observances.
*Upáyapratyaya.* A state of abstract meditation.
*Uttara-Gítá.* The name of a book supposed to be related by *Srí Krishna* for the further instruction of *Arjuna*.

*Uttara Mîmânsâ.* Another name for the *Vedânta* philosophy, written originally in the form of aphorisms by *Vyâsa.*

*Vach* or *Vâk.* lit. "Speech." The Word, the Logos.

*Vâda.* Argumentative knowledge.

*Vairâgyam.* Non-attachment to the attractions of the senses. Renunciation.

*Vaiśeshika.* A branch of the *Nyâya* school of philosophy; the Atomic school.

*Vaishnavas.* The followers or worshippers of *Vishnu,* who form one of the principal Hindu religious sects.

*Vâmadeva.* A great *Rishi* who possessed the highest spiritual enlightenment from the time of his birth.

*Vânaprastha.* The forest life. Third of the four stages into which the life of a man was divided in ancient India.

*Varâha-Purâna.* One of the eighteen principal *Puranas.*

*Vardhate.* To grow.

*Vârtikam.* A concise explanatory note.

*Varuna.* The old Vedic god of the sky.

*Vâsanâ.* A habit or tendency arising from an impression remaining unconsciously in the mind from past *Karma.*

*Vâsudeva.* Manifestation of the highest Being.

*Vâtsalya.* The affection of parents for children.

*Vâyu.* lit. "The vibrating." The air.

*Vedanâ.* The fine power of feeling developed by the *Yogî.*

*Vedas.* The Hindus Scriptures, consisting of the *Rig-Veda,* the *Yajur-Veda,* the *Sama-Veda,* the *Atharva-Veda;* also the *Brahmanas* and the *Upanishads;* comprising the hymns, rituals and philosophy of the Hindu religion.

*Vedânta.* The final philosophy of the *Vedas,* as expressed in the *Upanishads.* The philosophical system which embraces all Indian systems of philosophy, — the monistic, the mono-dualistic and the dualistic.

*Vêdâvai anantah.* A quotation from the *Vedas,* meaning "The Scriptures are infinite."

*Videha.* Science, or knowledge.

*Vidvân.* Disembodied, or unconscious of body.

*Vidyâ.* One who knows.

*Vijnâna.* The higher knowledge.

*Vikalpa.* Verbal delusion, doubt, notion, fancy.

*Vikaranabhâva.* Uninstrumental perception.

*Vikshipta.* A scattered or confused state of the mind.

*Vimoksha.* Absence of desire. Absolute freedom.

*Vinâ.* A stringed musical instrument of India.

# GLOSSARY 293

*Viparyaya.* False conception of a thing whose real form does not correspond to that conception, as mother of pearl mistaken for silver.
*Vipra.* A sage who was born and bred a Brahmin.
*Viraba.* Intense misery due to separation from the beloved one.
*Virya.* Strength, energy.
*Visbnu.* The "Preserver" of the Hindu trinity, who takes care of the universe, and who incarnates from time to time to help mankind.
*Viśisbtádvaita.* Qualified non-dualism. A school of Indian philosophy, founded by Râmânuja, a great religious reformer, which teaches that the individual soul is a part of God.
*Viśisbtádvaitin.* A follower of the above school of philosophy; a qualified non-dualist.
*Viśoka.* "Sorrowless."
*Vivekánanda.* "Bliss-in-discrimination."
*Vitarka.* Questioning or philosophical enquiry.
*Viveka.* Discrimination (of the true from the false).
*Viśuddba.* The fifth lotos of the *Yogîs,* opposite the throat (in the *Susbumná*).
*Vraja.* A suburb of the city of *Muttra,* where *Krisbna* played in his childhood.
*Vrindá.* The attendant of the principal *Gopî.*
*Vritti.* lit. "The whirlpool." Wave form in the *cbitta;* a modification of the mind.
*Vyána.* The nerve current which circulates all over the body.
*Vyása.* lit. "One who expands" (as a commentator). One *Vyása* was the author of the *Mabábbárata* and of the *Uttara Mímánsá.*
*Vyása Sutras.* The Vedânta Aphorisms by *Vyása.*
*Vyasti.* The particular (as opposed to the universal).
*Vyuttbána.* Waking, or returning to consciousness after abstract meditation.

*Yajur-Veda.* The ritualistic portion of the *Veda.*
*Yama.* The internal purification through moral training, preparatory to *Yoga.* The god of Death, so called from his power of self-control.
*Yoga.* Joining; union of the lower self with the higher self, by means of mental control. Any sort of culture that leads us to God.
*Yoga Sútra.* Aphorism on *Yoga.*
*Yogî.* One who practices *Yoga.*
*Yudbistbira.* A great Hindu Emperor who lived about 1400 B.C. He was one of the five *Pándavas.*
*Yuga.* A cycle or age of the world. The present cycle is known in India as the "*Kali-Yuga*" or "Iron-Age."

Printed in the USA
CPSIA information can be obtained
at www.ICGtesting.com
LVHW041918031023
759781LV00061B/993